A Tale of Four Augusts

Obama's Syria Policy

A Tale of Four Augusts
Obama's Syria Policy

KILIC BUGRA KANAT

SETA

Ankara 2015

KILIC BUGRA KANAT | Kilic Bugra Kanat is an Assistant Professor of Political Science at Penn State University, Erie and a research scholar at the SETA Foundation at Washington, D.C. He received his doctoral degree in Political Science from Syracuse University. He holds a master's degree in Political Science from Syracuse University and a master's in International Affairs from Marquette University. He completed his undergraduate education in the International Relations Department of the Middle East Technical University. Dr. Kanat also holds a Certificate of Advanced Studies in Middle Eastern Affairs and Certificate of Advanced Graduate Study in Conflict Resolution. His research interests include foreign policy decision-making, foreign policy change, and domestic politics and foreign policy interaction. He was also selected for the Future Leaders Program of Foreign Policy Initiative. Dr. Kanat's writings have appeared in Foreign Policy, The Diplomat, Insight Turkey, Middle East Policy, Arab Studies Quarterly, Mediterranean Quarterly, Journal of Balkan and Near Eastern Studies, and Journal of Muslim Minority Affairs. He is a columnist for Daily Sabah. He is also co-editor of an edited volume – History, Politics and Foreign Policy in Turkey – published by the SETA Foundation.

SETA Publications 4
First Published in 2015 by SETA
ISBN: 978-605-4023-52-3

© 2015 SET Vakfı İktisadi İşletmesi

Cover and Layout: Ümare Yazar
Printed in Turkey, İstanbul by Turkuvaz Matbaacılık Yayıncılık A.Ş., March 2015

SETA Publications
Nenehatun Caddesi No: 66 GOP Çankaya 06700 Ankara Turkey
Tel:+90 312.551 21 00 | Fax :+90 312.551 21 90
www.setav.org | kitap@setav.org

Cover Photo: US President Barack Obama speaks about Syria from the Rose Garden at the White House in Washington, DC, on August 31, 2013. AFP / Jim Watson

TABLE OF CONTENTS

ACKNOWLEDGMENTS   7

INTRODUCTION   9

ONE   THE BUSH YEARS
        (2001-2008)   15

TWO   THAWING RELATIONS BEFORE THE ARAB SPRING
        (FEBRUARY 2009-MARCH 2011)   29

        Stability in Iraq   45
        Middle East Peace   50
        Non-Proliferation   57

THREE   THE ARAB SPRING THUNDERS THROUGH SYRIA
        (MARCH 2011-AUGUST 2011)   65

FOUR   OBAMA CALLS FOR ASSAD'S REMOVAL
        (AUGUST 2011-AUGUST 2012)   77

FIVE   OBAMA'S RED LINE
        (AUGUST 2012-AUGUST 2013)   97

SIX   A NEW CALCULUS
        (AUGUST 2013-AUGUST 2014)   115

SEVEN   CONCLUSION
        ISIS AND THE NEW ERA IN U.S. POLICY ON SYRIA   143

TIMELINE OF U.S.-SYRIA RELATIONS
(JANUARY 2009 TO JUNE 2014)   147

ACKNOWLEDGMENTS

I would like to thank Erol Cebeci for his support during the writing of this report. Kadir Ustun's comments and edits have been very helpful. Sally Judson edited several versions of this study. I also warmly thank Erica Hanichak for her contribution to the report through her extensive research. Her insight into the evolution of the administration's Syria policy was invaluable.

INTRODUCTION

The Syrian conflict that began as a revolution quickly descended into a major humanitarian disaster with the Assad regime's increasing use of force and the militarization of the dispute between the regime and the opposition. The complexity of the civil war has led the international community to abandon the country due to a growing reluctance by Western countries, including the U.S., to engage in the conflict despite the gross violation of human rights and constant breach of international norms and principles. The country is witnessing a gloomy reality on the ground and there is little evidence to suggest any breakthrough in the near future. The ever-growing death toll, thousands of documented cases of war crimes and systematic torture, the use of weapons of mass destruction and the rise of radical groups have all failed to stir a robust American response. The U.S. did not change its stance until August 2014, when two American journalists, James Foley and Steven Sotloff, were violently beheaded by the Islamic State of Iraq and Syria (ISIS). Even then President Obama's strategy only entailed plans to "degrade" and "destroy" ISIS, with very little reference to the future of Syria or the Assad regime.

So far, President Obama's new strategy has been almost unanimously considered ineffective to eliminate ISIS from the region. It fails to provide comfort and peace for the Syrian people and stability to the region. Even after the airstrikes began, very little had changed in the lives of ordinary Syrians. The formation of the international coalition was not meant to end the brutality of the Assad regime, which is the root cause of the emergence and rise of radical groups in Syria. Even the most optimist analysts in Washington, DC project that U.S. policy will only change after the departure of the Obama administration in 2016 and the election of a new president. For many that we interviewed in Washington, DC, including observers of U.S. foreign policy on Syria and former members of the administration, the most significant determinant of U.S. policy on Syria has been the opinion of Obama's inner circle, a few close advisers. The position of these individuals closely matches the worldview and foreign policy vision of President Obama, who, along with his inner circle, determined the U.S.'s Syria policy, sometimes without consulting major figures and actors in the absence of any interagency process.

With the culmination of events in Syria, the Syrian public feels that it has been forsaken by the U.S. given its apparent neglect or even deliberate abandonment despite President Obama's statement about Assad in August 2011. A clear reality concerning U.S. foreign policy in Syria has emerged after four Augusts of inaction, indecisiveness and a lack of strategy. These policy inefficiencies greatly contributed to the deterioration of the situation on the ground, bringing Syria into the nightmare scenario that frightened and worried many actors in the region. The past four years speak to the tribulations in Syria. The regime employed SCUD missiles, barrel bombs, chemical weapons, and committed crimes against humanity and war crimes. Although the extent of the tragedy approached that seen in Rwanda and the lawlessness nearly mirrored Somalia, the U.S. administration did not foresee any possible security fallouts from Syria until ISIS became a major threat.

This report provides a synopsis of the past four years of U.S. policy in Syria. It brings together the major turning points of this policy since the beginning of the Arab Spring and positions that different actors endorsed since 2009. The first section is dedicated to explaining President Obama's attempt to restore ties with the Syrian government after the 2008 Presidential Election in order to resolve the foreign fighters problem in Iraq. This effort was also aimed at launching a subsequent peace process between Arab states and Israel as well as the issue of weapons of mass destruction. Despite opposition from Congress and some segments of Washington, President Obama appointed an ambassador to Damascus and official talks were launched during his first two years in office. However, this process was disrupted by the Arab Spring and the Assad regime's heavy-handed response towards the demonstrations. Particularly, the use of force during some demonstrations and the increasing number of casualties drove the U.S. to change its course of action in its relations with Syria.

Following the Assad regime's forceful action against the peaceful demonstrations and after much deliberation, President Obama took a major step forward in the U.S.'s policy towards Syria in August 2011. He stated, "For the sake of the Syrian people, the time has come for President Assad to step aside."[1] At that time, this was interpreted as a first step towards a comprehensive action plan to overthrow the regime in Syria, which would include using force against the regime and aiding rebel groups. However, this expectation soon proved to be misguided, as the U.S. preferred to follow a policy of inaction. The administration appeared to be indecisive about the next step. The message of "Assad must go" was given to avoid missing the possible overthrow of the regime and in the name of "being on the right side of history," instead of a result of a policy planning process.

An additional major turning point took place when President Obama made a statement in August 2012 in response to a question about the rumors that the Assad regime was moving chemical weapons. He stated that U.S. policy towards the conflict would be revised should there be any attempt or evidence that the Syrian regime was prepared to use chemical weapons. He said, "We have been very clear to the Assad regime, but also to other players on the ground that a red line for us is when we start seeing a whole bunch of chemical weapons moving around or being utilized. That would change my calculus...That would change my equation...We're monitoring that situation very carefully. We have put together a range of contingency plans."[2] This statement was again interpreted as a sign that

[1] Scott Wilson and Joby Warrick, "Assad Must Go, Obama Say," *The Washington Post,* August 18, 2011, http://www.washingtonpost.com/politics/assad-must-go-obama-says/2011/08/18/gIQAelheOJ_story.html.

[2] James Ball, "Obama Issues Syria a 'Red Line' Warning on Chemical Weapons," *The Washington Post,* August 20 2012, http://www.washingtonpost.com/world/national-security/obama-issues-syria-red-line-warning-on-chemical-weapons/2012/08/20/ba5d26ec-eaf7-11e1-b811-09036bcb182b_story.html.

the U.S. was prepared to take decisive action to stop the Assad regime from employing chemical weapons. However, U.S. actions following the statement were not sufficient to deter the Assad regime from using these weapons. In the period following this statement, there were several reports confirming the use of chemical weapons by the Assad regime against the opposition and civilians in different parts of Syria. The first of such an attack was reported in December of 2012, but there was no U.S. response to deter the Syrian regime from further chemical weapons usage.[3]

The third significant development in U.S. policy was President Obama's "red line" speech, when the Assad regime used chemical weapons in the town of Ghoutta near Damascus in August 2013, exactly a year after President Obama's "red line" statement. Many around the globe expected a rapid U.S. reaction that would include military strikes, leading to the overthrow of the Syrian regime. However, President Obama's initial statements underlined that military strikes would not target the regime and the mission in question would not be aimed at overthrowing the Assad regime. Instead, Obama explained that it would be limited to destroying the capability of the Syrian regime to launch subsequent chemical weapon attacks. Even then, many analysts indicated that the U.S. administration was very reluctant to take the necessary steps to achieve this limited goal. President Obama's decision to seek Congressional approval, in the wake of British Prime Minister Cameron's resolve to seek authorization from the UK parliament, was regarded as another sign of this reluctant position. Later, the plan quickly took a U-turn as a direct result of Russian intervention. President Obama decided to refrain from launching the attack, to the dismay of the international community and an angered Syrian opposition. As it will be argued below, the shift frustrated both the Syrian opposition and U.S. allies in the region because of the confusion it created and the lack of a communication or deliberation with U.S. allies during the decision-making process.

[3]Robert Johnson and Geoffrey Ingersoll, " 'Poison Gas Bombs' in Syria Could Force US Intervention," *Business Insider,* December 24, 2012, http://www.businessinsider.com/assad-reportedly-using-chemical-weapons-homs-syria-rebels-2012-12.

Meanwhile, radical groups were gaining further ground in Syria. While the U.S. ignored calls for action from the international community, ISIS began surpassing other rebel groups in Syria in numbers and capabilities and launching operations to destabilize Iraq. At the beginning of 2014, when asked about the potential impact of radical groups in Syria and particularly those who were affiliated with Al-Qaida, President Obama referred to them as jayvee teams and clearly underemphasized the disruptive impact that they could generate in the region. The group captured Mosul, the second largest city in Iraq, in June 2014. When the group laid a siege on Erbil, the U.S. began to act to protect U.S. servicemen and civilians in the city. Later in August 2014, when ISIS beheaded two American journalists, the Obama administration announced a plan to form an international coalition to "degrade" and "destroy" ISIS.

The following chapters will serve to illuminate U.S. policy in Syria over the last four years. Chapters 1 and 2 provide context for the Obama administration's treatment of the Syrian civil war by analyzing the status of relations in the years preceding the conflict. They conclude that the Obama administration worked cohesively to try to reverse George W. Bush's deliberate antagonizing of the Syrian regime and to launch a rapprochement with Assad to achieve its main goals in the Middle East. Chapters 3 through 6 address U.S.-Syrian relations since the Arab Spring and demonstrate the chokehold that risk aversion has held over the Obama administration despite ample, if imperfect, opportunities to strengthen the Syrian opposition and foster a possible transition to democracy in Syria. The final chapter will assess what changes, if any, stakeholders may expect in U.S. Syria policy during the Obama administration's remaining two years.

ONE THE BUSH YEARS
(2001-2008)

“ U.S. foreign policy under George
W. Bush represented one of the most
complicated periods of U.S.-Syrian
relations in recent history.

U.S. foreign policy under George W. Bush represented one of the most complicated periods of U.S.-Syrian relations in recent history. Especially after 9/11, relations between the two countries became complex. First, the Bush administration's willingness to target not only terrorist organizations, but also states that were allegedly sponsoring terrorism after the 9/11 attacks generated a high degree of anxiety about Syria. In his address to the nation on the night of September 11, 2001, President Bush stated that the United States "will make no distinction between the terrorists who committed these acts and those who harbor them."[4] This was an important issue for Syria as it had been on the United States' list of states sponsoring terrorism since 1979 mostly due to its direct support for Hezbollah. However, the Syrian government acted quickly to join the U.S. War on Terror by providing valuable intelligence in regards to different groups emerging in the Middle East.

According to former American military and diplomatic officials, in early 2002, Syria became one of the CIA's most effective intelligence allies in the fight against terrorism.[5] Accordingly, the Syrian regime compiled a large amount of intelligence about al-Qaeda fighters, cells and recruiters operating in the Middle East and Europe. Syrian intelligence was extremely valuable for U.S. counter-terrorism operations, especially in Germany. Furthermore, Syria also began providing access for the FBI and CIA to

[4]George W. Bush: "Address to the Nation on the Terrorist Attacks," September 11, 2001 (online by Gerhard Peters and John T. Woolley, The American Presidency Project) http://www.presidency.ucsb.edu/ws/?pid=58057.

[5]Seymour M. Hersh, "The Syrian Bet," The New Yorker, July 28, 2003, http://www.newyorker.com/magazine/2003/07/28/the-syrian-bet.

launch intelligence-gathering operations in Aleppo. Some of the information provided by the Syrian regime to the U.S. was actionable intelligence. For example, in one case, Syrian intelligence reportedly detected
that al-Qaeda was preparing a USS Cole type of attack on the U.S. Navy in
Bahrain through a glider loaded with explosives that would be flown into
the headquarters. Syria provided the news to the United States, effectively
aiding the U.S. in thwarting the attack. In addition to providing intelligence, Syria also assisted the U.S. in preventing an attack on an American target in the Canadian capital, Ottawa.[6] In the meantime, Syria also
became an important destination for those detained by U.S, forces in its
war against terrorism. A great many of these detainees were transferred to
Syria in order to be interrogated and tortured by Syrian officers within the
extraordinary rendition program, who then sent any information acquired
through interrogations to the U.S. government.[7]

In the early phase of the War on Terror, the Syrian regime attempted to
turn the crisis into an opportunity. At the end of the day, it perceived this as a
chance to improve relations with the United States. The War on Terror could
prove extremely instrumental to convince the U.S. to remove Syria from the
list of countries sponsoring terrorism.[8] This would allow the Syrian regime
to earn international legitimacy and to be considered a "normal nation" in
a crisis-ridden Middle East. Secondly, if used properly, Syria could label domestic dissent—in particular, the Muslim Brotherhood of Syria— as terrorism and gain international support for its operations against these groups.
This would strengthen the government, as a tool of deterrence, vis-à-vis any
groups that dared to stand against the Syrian regime.

However, mutual relations grew sour after the U.S. invaded Iraq. Syria
opposed the operation, and after it became clear that the U.S. would not

[6]Hersh, "The Syrian Bet."

[7]Ian Cobain, "CIA Rendition: More than a Quarter of Countries 'Offered Covert Support,'"
The Guardian, February 5, 2013, http://www.theguardian.com/world/2013/feb/05/cia-rendi-
tion-countries-covert-support.

[8]Hersh, "The Syrian Bet."

go back on its decision, Syria ceased to provide intelligence and ended any cooperation with the U.S. against Al-Qaeda. Syria acted together with the U.S. in the UN Security Council (UNSC) by voting for Resolution 1441, demanding that Iraq permit the renewal of the UN supervisors' work. However, this support was explained by Damascus as an attempt to stop the warfare between Iraq and the United States.[9] Damascus was openly against any military attack against or invasion of Iraq. The leaders of the regime, including Bashar al-Assad and Foreign Minister Faruq al-Sahara, openly denounced the invasion plan. During an interview, Assad stated, "No doubt the U.S. is a superpower capable of conquering a relatively small country, but the U.S. and Britain are incapable of controlling all of Iraq."[10] Meanwhile, Syria's Grand Mufti, Ahmad Kaftaru, asked Muslims "to use all means and martyrdom operations to defeat the American, British and Zionist aggression on Iraq."[11] Simultaneously, the Syrian regime let the public freely criticize and demonstrate against the United States. During this period, a key factor generating this level of concern among the Syrian regime in regards to the invasion were rumors that once the U.S. was done with Iraq, Syria would be the next target. [12]

In the immediate aftermath of the Iraq invasion, relations between the two countries deteriorated.[13] First, reports showed that Syria was allowing foreign fighters to transit through its territories into Iraq.[14] Intelligence agencies reported that almost 80 percent of foreign fighters in Iraq flew

[9]Moshe Ma'oz, "Washington and Damascus: Between Confrontation and Cooperation," *United States Institute of Peace Special Report* 146 (2005): http://www.usip.org/sites/default/files/sr146.pdf.

[10]Raymond Hinnebusch, "Defying the Hegemon: Syria and the Iraqi War" (paper presented at the European Consortium on Political Research conference, Budapest, Hungary, September 2005) https://www.st-andrews.ac.uk/media/school-of-international-relations/mecacs/workingpapers/defying_the_hegemon.pdf.

[11]Ibid.

[12]Alfred B. Prados and Jeremy M. Sharp, "Syria: Political Conditions and Relations with the United States After the Iraqi War," *CRS Report for Congress,* January 10, 2005, http://fpc.state.gov/documents/organization/42483.pdf.

[13]Wallsh, "Syrian Alliance Strategy in the Post-Cold War Era."

[14]BS

through Damascus to join the insurgency.[15] These fighters joined Sunni groups, particularly al-Qaeda in Iraq (AQI), which posed the most substantial challenge to U.S. efforts to stabilize the country. Although the Syrian government denied any link with these groups, employees of the U.S. Embassy in Damascus reported that they often witnessed pro-al-Qaeda rallies in front of the embassy compound, a situation that they believed could only occur with the tacit consent of the Syrian regime.[16] Moreover, in 2004, the Bush administration handed the Syrian government a list of 34 operatives based in Syria that were suspected of involvement in the insurgency in Iraq as well as in the 9/11 terrorist attacks. Yet, the Syrian government detained only one operative from the entire list, which fostered a growing distrust of Damascus in Washington.[17] After mounting pressure in February 2005, Syria handed over the stepbrother of Saddam Hussein and deported a number of foreign fighter recruiters to North African countries.[18] However, that was not enough to persuade the U.S. about Syria.

There was disagreement among Bush administration officials over how to counter the flow of fighters heading to Iraq from Syria. The director of the CIA at the time, David Petraeus, proposed going to Damascus and personally confronting Bashar al-Assad face-to-face. Journalist Peter Baker cited Petraeus' colloquial description of Assad's actions: "You're basically allowing poisonous snakes to have a nest in your country with the understanding they only bite the neighbors' kids and sooner or later that backfires and they end up biting your kids and then they do worse." Assad signaled that he was willing to meet with Petraeus in order to gain some degree of legitimacy, despite the awkwardness of the President meeting

---

[15]Peter Baker, *Days of Fire: Bush and Cheney in the White House* (New York, Anchor Press, 2014), 557.

[16]Interview by Kilic Kanat, July 2014.

[17]Robin Wright, "U.S. and UN Step Up Pressure on Damascus," *The Washington Post*, February 16, 2005, http://www.washingtonpost.com/wp-dyn/articles/A26044-2005Feb15.html.

[18]Hinnebusch, "Defying the Hegemon."

with the commander of U.S. forces in Iraq, which were considered invaders by the same regime. However, officials in the White House refused to engage in dialogue with the Syrian regime at such a high level without Damascus taking significant steps towards meeting U.S. demands.[19] The more hawkish members of the administration, including then Deputy National Security Advisor Elliott Abrams, went a step further by arguing that dialogue was futile and recommending military action against the airport in Damascus to stem the flow of foreign fighters.[20] Although the Bush administration did not attack the Damascus airport, there were limited military strikes by the U.S. inside Syria. For instance, in June 2003, U.S. troops attacked a convoy of military vehicles within Syrian territory, which resulted in the death of Syrian soldiers, infuriating the Syrian regime and creating further dismay in Damascus.[21]

The issue of foreign fighters was not the sole predicament between the two countries in regards to Iraq. After the occupation of Iraq by U.S. forces and the subsequent foundation of a new Iraqi government, numerous additional factors began to generate complications. For instance, the two countries disagreed over the newly created and U.S.-supported Iraq Governing Council. Syria opposed this structure, campaigning to rally the opposition against it. Soon afterward, the Syrian government finally voted affirmatively for the recognition of the Iraqi Governing Council and restored its diplomatic relations with Iraq. However, the low intensity crisis between Syria and U.S. persisted. There was also a disagreement between Baghdad and Damascus over the fate of Iraqi funds transferred to Syria prior to the invasion. The Iraqi Governing Council requested that the funds be returned from Syria; however, the Syrian government insisted that they were payments for Syrian businessmen.[22] In response to this growing crisis

---

[19]Michael Gordon, *The Endgame: The Inside Story of the Struggle for Iraq from George W. Bush to Barack Obama* (New York: Vintage Press, 2014), 462.

[20]Baker, 558.

[21]Ma'oz, "Washington and Damascus."

[22]Hinnebusch, "Defying the Hegemon."

between the neighboring countries, President Bush signed HR 1828, *The Syria Accountability and Lebanese Sovereignty Act*. This act imposed penalties on Syria "unless it ceases support for international terrorist groups, ends its occupation of Lebanon, ceases the development weapons of mass destruction, (WMD), and has ceased supporting or facilitating terrorist activity in Iraq."[23] These sanctions included bans on selling military items and dual use items to Syria. Furthermore, in the late phase of the Iraq War, the White House Freedom Agenda, along with the Bush administration's attempts to overthrow authoritarian regimes and build democracies in the Middle East, also caused increasing concern in Syria.[24] For many in Damascus, this new agenda generated the expectation that the U.S. would target additional Arab states with authoritarian governments following the fall of the Saddam regime.

While the developments in Iraq and increasing tensions between Syria and the U.S. generated a significant impasse, the assassination of Rafik al-Hariri, the former Prime Minister of Lebanon, on February 14, 2005 would bring relations between the United States and Syria to a new low.[25] The Lebanon rift in relations has been a long-standing schism. For decades, the U.S. and Western countries requested that the Syrian regime pull its troops from Lebanese soil. However, with the Iraqi crisis, this pressure reached a new high. Although Syria pulled some of its troops in 2003, a significant number of soldiers remained with the capacity to play a significant and determinative role in the country. Later in 2004, under the leadership of the United States, the UN Security Council passed Resolution 1559 calling Syria to withdraw its forces from Lebanon.[26] However, Syria did not comply and continued to intervene in Lebanese domestic affairs,

---

[23]Prados and Sharp, "Syria: Political Conditions and Relations with the United States After the Iraqi War."

[24]"Fact Sheet: President Bush's Freedom Agenda Helped Protect The American People," The White House, http://georgewbush-whitehouse.archives.gov/infocus/freedomagenda/.

[25]Jeremy Sharp, "Syria: Background and U.S. Relations," *Congressional Research Service*, April 26, 2010, 13; Hersh, "The Syrian Bet," 7.

[26]Ma'oz, "Washington and Damascus."

leading to the resignation of al-Hariri in protest. After a few months later, he was assassinated in Beirut.

The United States, along with most Western countries at the time, believed Syria was accountable for the assassination and ratcheted up criticism of the Assad regime. In a news conference, Secretary of State Condoleezza Rice claimed that U.S. national security interests had begun to diverge significantly from those of the Syrian government and noted, "The Syrian government is unfortunately on a path right now where relations are not improving but are worsening."[27] The administration was careful not to link the Syrian government directly with the assassination, but most statements from high-ranking U.S. officials subtly implicated Damascus. Rice signaled Syria's culpability in an address to the international community: "When something happens in Lebanon, Syria needs to help to find accountability for what has happened there. There is a part of the destabilization that takes place when you have the kind of conditions that you do now in Lebanon thanks to Syrian interference."[28] Outraged, the U.S. government withdrew Ambassador Margaret Scobey in the days following the assassination.

The Hariri assassination altered the United States' understanding of the Levant, as decision-makers would thereafter find it impossible to ignore Syria's role in Lebanese instability. Bush demanded that Syria disentangle itself from Lebanese politics, calling for the country to "withdraw its troops and secret services from Lebanon so as to allow Lebanon's upcoming elections to be held freely."[29] Tension with Syria escalated in the weeks following this declaration as Assad showed little remorse for his country's involvement in the Hariri assassination or in Lebanon's failed attempts at democratic consolidation. Former Syrian regime official Bassam Barabandi wrote that Bashar al-Assad had ordered his subordinates to do whatever

[27] Wright, "U.S. and UN Step Up Pressure on Damascus."

[28] Ibid.

[29] Andrew Tabler, *In the Lion's Den: An Eyewitness Account of Washington's Battle with Syria* (Chicago: Chicago Review Press, 2011), 84.

necessary to obstruct investigations, whether by stalling the legal process, using Hezbollah to apply pressure on Lebanon, or fomenting violence in Iraq as a way to distract the international community.[30] Borrowing a page from his father's playbook, Assad encouraged regional instability to create problems for which he was the only solution, thereby making his regime more relevant to global powers. Still, Assad's posturing did not convince the White House that he no longer posed a threat to the Freedom Agenda. Instead, Lebanon's reaction to Syrian interference in the wake of the Hariri assassination only served to embolden the Bush administration's condemnation of Assad and commitment to its program of democracy promotion.[31] The United States was joined by France and the UN in its calls for Syria to back down, which proved effective on March 5, 2005, when Bashar al-Assad announced that Syria would implement its gradual and organized withdrawal from Lebanon.[32] Though Syrian capitulation on the issue of troop withdrawal demonstrated a modicum of good faith, Assad's ongoing support of Hezbollah prevented any meaningful progress on the status of U.S.-Syria relations.

Syria's reported nuclear activities remained the third source of tension in bilateral relationship. As Former Secretary of Defense Robert Gates described in his memoirs, reports from Israeli intelligence services in spring 2007 uncovered compelling evidence that North Korea aided Syria in building a facility capable of producing plutonium for nuclear weapons. This information generated a great discussion among U.S. officials on strategies to push Syria to halt its nuclear program. According to Gates' account, some officials in the administration, such as Vice President Dick Cheney, believed that U.S. interests were best served by launching military

---

[30]Bassam Barabandi and Tyler Jess Thompson, "Inside Assad's Playbook: Time and Terror," *MENA* Source (Atlantic Council blog), July 23, 2014, http://www.atlanticcouncil.org/blogs/menasource/inside-assad-s-playbook-time-and-terror.

[31]Baker, 383.

[32]"A Death in the Middle East: Hariri's Murder Casts Uncertain Future for Lebanon," *Spiegel*, February 24, 2005, http://www.spiegel.de/international/a-death-in-the-middle-east-hariri-s-murder-casts-uncertain-future-for-lebanon-a-343485.html.

strikes on the facility: not only would strikes destroy the facility and crip-
ple the program but they would also send a powerful signal to the other
countries with nuclear aspirations, especially Syria's ally, Iran.[33] There were
others, like Elliott Abrams, who advocated leaving a military response up
to Israel, which was eager to demonstrate its military might after it failed
to conclusively end its war with Lebanon in 2006.[34] Still, others advocated doing nothing because they believed the United States had enough
problems fighting the wars in Iraq and Afghanistan and were not eager to
start a third, particularly when the Bush administration was facing heavy
criticism for the faulty intelligence that led to the invasion of Iraq. Moreover, these officials were reticent to cooperate militarily with Israel against
an Arab country for fear of inflaming regional tensions. One final camp,
which included Robert Gates, advocated implementing a diplomatic initiative that would dismantle the facility without the use of force.[35] Nevertheless, these policy debates became a moot point when Israel decided to
strike the facility unilaterally. It is still unclear how much the U.S. knew
prior to the attacks, but it was a welcome solution.

In fact, in the midst of all these crises, some individuals in the Bush
administration began to advocate for unilaterally attacking Syria because
of its nuclear facilities and/or because of its active support for the insurgency in Iraq. Bilateral relations were minimal despite some level of dialogue to stop the flow of foreign fighters. During this period, the U.S.
did everything in its disposal to hurt the Assad regime. It was clear that
the country was experiencing rather serious difficulties. The imposition of
harsh economic sanctions and withdrawal of the U.S. ambassador greatly
alienated the country, which was already facing growing international reproach. George W. Bush rejected domestic and international pressure to
engage Syria as a way to advance the Arab-Israeli peace process because he

[33]Robert Gates, *Duty : Memoirs of a Secretary at War* (New York: Alfred A. Knopf. New York, 2014), 384.

[34]Baker, 552.

[35]Gates, 387.

feared such a move would undermine Syria's global isolation.[36] Instead, he declared that "it would be counterproductive" to engage Syria in talks, as "Syria knows exactly what it takes to get better relations."[37]

During this period, all branches of the U.S. government were acting in concert to isolate the Syrian regime. Not only had the U.S. Congress passed the 2003 *Syria Accountability and Restoration of Lebanese Sovereignty Act*, which had damaging repercussions on the Syrian regime's economy. The White House also declared a national emergency in respect to Syria in May 2004, which harshened economic sanctions in reaction to Syria's support for different armed groups in the Middle East.[38] The same year, the Department of Treasury designated the Commercial Bank of Syria "a financial institution of primary money laundering concern" and passed another set of sanctions against Syria.[39] This new set of sanctions had a significant impact on the economic relations of Syria. It limited "Syria's ability to carry out activities involving U.S. currency or repatriate its oil revenues while simultaneously dissuading foreign entities from commercial dealings with Syria."[40] Targeted sanctions were implemented to freeze the financial assets of Syrian agencies and high-level officials. These sanctions, combined with George Bush's declaration of democracy promotion and freedom agenda, transformed the nature of the countries' relationship. Syria no longer merely viewed U.S. actions as hostile, but considered them an existential threat. Likewise, the Bush administration regarded Assad's government a "rogue regime" that could endanger U.S. national security interests.

[36]International Crisis Group, "Restarting Israeli-Syrian Negotiations," *Middle East Report No 63*, April 10, 2007, http://www.crisisgroup.org/en/regions/middle-east-north-africa/israel-palestine/063-restarting-israeli-syrian-negotiations.aspx.

[37]Barrack Obama, "Remarks by the President on the Global War on Terror," April 20, 2007 (online by U.S. Department of State) http://2001-2009.state.gov/r/pa/ei/wh/83362.htm.

[38]BS. P.61

[39]BS. P 62

[40]International Crisis Group, "Engaging Syria? U.S. Constraints and Opportunities," *Middle East Report No. 83*, February 11, 2009, http://www.crisisgroup.org/~/media/Files/Middle%20East%20North%20Africa/Iraq%20Syria%20Lebanon/Syria/83engagingsyriausconstraintsandopportunities.ashx.

There were several exceptions to the U.S. policy of isolating Syria during this period, including several meetings between U.S. officials and their Syrian counterparts. One significant visit was conducted by Nancy Pelosi, who assumed the position of the Speaker of the House of Representatives after the midterm elections in 2006. In April 2007, Pelosi, despite some protests and opposition from the Bush administration, visited Damascus as part of her Middle East tour. After the meeting, Pelosi underlined U.S. concerns about Syrian support for Hamas and Hezbollah and expressed the necessity of launching a peace process between Israel and Syria.[41] However, despite these statements, the trip was harshly criticized by the Bush administration. President Bush affirmed that visiting Damascus in such a critical juncture meant sending mixed messages to the international community. He also stressed that there were several other similar attempts by officials from different branches of government; however, those failed owing to the fact that the Assad regime did not take any meaningful steps in areas of international concern.[42]

Just days before the U.S. presidential elections in November 2008, another development strained relations between the two countries. After tensions between the two peaked in regards to foreign fighters in Iraq, the U.S. acted unilaterally and attacked several targets within Syria under the premise that they were providing recruitment and training support for the ongoing insurgency in Iraq. On October 26, 2008, U.S. Special Forces launched an operation in the Syrian town of Abu Kamal in an effort to destroy key logistic networks that facilitated the passage of foreign fighters from Syria into Iraq.[43] Special Forces targeted Badran Turki

[41]Hassan M. Fattah and Graham Bowley, "Pelosi Meets with Syrian Leader," *The New York Times*, April 4, 2007, http://www.nytimes.com/2007/04/04/world/middleeast/04cnd-pelosi.html?_r=0.

[42]"Bush Criticizes Pelosi's Trip to Syria," *The New York Times*, April 3, 2007, http://www.nytimes.com/2007/04/03/world/americas/03iht-web-0403bushap.5128610.html.

[43]Ian Black and Ewen MacAskill, "US Forces Kill Eight in Helicopter Raid on Syria," *The Guardian*, October 26, 2008, http://www.theguardian.com/world/2008/oct/27/syria-helicopter-attack.

Hishan al-Mazidih, also known as Abu Ghadiya, who was known to be a Syrian commander of AQI. According to U.S. sources, Abu Ghadiya "oversaw a network of training camps, including those run by more secular former Baath insurgents; he also met regularly with Syrian military intelligence officials, including Asif Shawkat, the country's intelligence chief and brother-in-law to President Bashar al-Assad."[44] Connecting the Syrian government with al-Qaeda was viewed as a serious accusation against Damascus. Unsurprisingly, the Syrian regime strongly denied the allegations. Eight people were killed in this unprecedented U.S. incursion into Syrian territory; however, Syrian sources denied Abu Ghadiya's presence in Abu Kamal and instead accused the United States of violating Syrian sovereignty and perpetrating state terror.[45] Although some news networks accused the Syrian government of cooperating with the United States by allowing the attack on the Abu Ghadiya network, this information was never confirmed, leading many to consider the attack a serious escalation in U.S. hostility towards Syria.[46] In response to the attack, the Syrian government summoned the U.S. *chargé d'affaires*, Maura Connelly, and subsequently shut down U.S.-operated facilities such as language schools and cultural centers.[47] Friction between the United States and Syria after the Abu Kamal raid inflamed existing tensions and made it clear by 2008 that the bilateral relationship had reached the nadir of its history.

[44]Gordon et.al, 230.

[45]Ann Scott Tyson and Ellen Knickmeyer, "U.S. Calls Raid a Warning to Syria," *The Washington Post,* October 28, 2008, http://www.washingtonpost.com/wp-dyn/content/article/2008/10/27/AR2008102700511.html; "US Helicopter Raid Inside Syria," *BBC News,* October 27, 2008, http://news.bbc.co.uk/2/hi/middle_east/7692153.stm.

[46]Dominic Waghorn, "Syria 'Gave Green Light For Raid,'" *Sky News,* October 28, 2008, http://news.sky.com/story/644001/syria-gave-green-light-for-raid.

[47]"US Helicopter Raid Inside Syria."

TWO THAWING RELATIONS BEFORE THE ARAB SPRING (FEBRUARY 2009-MARCH 2011)

❝ The U.S. hoped to encourage Syria to deny foreign fighters safe passage into Iraq, to distance itself from Iran, and to contribute more constructively to the Arab-Israeli peace negotiations by cutting funding to Hamas and Hezbollah.

"In terms of the Syrian-American relationship, the United States is committed to a dialogue based on mutual interest and mutual respect and a solid foundation for discussion of our shared goals and of real differences..."[48]

US Envoy George Mitchell, July 26, 2009

Prior to stepping foot in the Oval Office, Barack Obama began formulating his policy on Syria when he sent a delegation to Damascus in November 2008 to assess the status of U.S.-Syrian relations.[49] From that meeting, it became clear that Syria would be critical for the President-Elect's major foreign policy goals in the Middle East: a smooth U.S/ withdrawal from Iraq, containment of Iran's regional ambitions and a comprehensive Middle East Peace.[50] Key players throughout the inter-agency—from Assistant to the President of National Security Affairs James Jones to Secretary of State Hillary Clinton and Chair of the Senate Foreign Relations Committee John Kerry—believed that only direct communication with the Syrian government could convince its leader to cooperate with the United States. Specifically, the U.S. hoped to encourage Syria to deny foreign fighters safe passage into Iraq, to distance itself from Iran, and to contribute more constructively to the Arab-Israeli peace negotiations by cutting funding to Hamas and Hezbollah.[51] In the long term, Syria's

---

[48]"Obama's Middle East envoy steps up diplomatic push in Syria," *The Guardian,* July 26, 2009, http://www.theguardian.com/world/2009/jul/26/george-mitchell-syria-peace-talks.

[49]Bassel Oudat, "Ping-pong Diplomacy," *Al-Ahram,* No. 923 (November 2008): http://weekly.ahram.org.eg/2008/923/re6.htm.

[50]Interview by Kilic Kanat, July 2014.

[51]Steven Heydemann, interview by Kilic Kanat, January 2015.

support of these U.S. foreign policy endeavors was thought to be critical in realizing the Obama administration's goal of gradually disengaging from the conflict-prone politics of the region. Though the Obama administration faced push back from lawmakers in Washington and the American public, it hoped that the Syrian government would be receptive to warmer relations. However, under these circumstances and after decades of tension between the two countries, the first step would be hard to take. For President Obama and his administration, this first step would have to be resuming diplomatic relations at a time where they were at their frostiest.

President Obama, having very little leverage over Syria absent diplomatic representation and economic trade, had to forge a new path for U.S. engagement in the Middle East. Syria welcomed the Obama administration in 2009 with an eagerness for engagement unparalleled in the history of the countries' bilateral ties.[52] In fact, Assad had viewed the 2008 presidential election as an opportunity to change the course of the countries' relationship.[53] Upon Obama's victory and without any sign of rapprochement yet, Assad expressed content with the election results. In a statement after the elections, Assad revealed that he was actually following the U.S. elections quite closely and emphasized, "We are happy that [Obama] has said that diplomacy—and not war—is the means of conducting international policy."[54] The U.S. elections were important not only due to Obama's emphasis on diplomacy, but also because they marked the end of an administration that was prominently known for its use of direct military intervention to change regimes.

Immediately after the election, numerous articles and commentaries appeared in the Syrian media, known to be controlled by the Assad regime, in favor of establishing better relations with the United States. Under the leadership of Assad and with the strict censorship of the Syrian

[52]Seymour Hersh, "Syria Calling," *The New Yorker,* April 6, 2009, http://www.newyorker.com/magazine/2009/04/06/syria-calling, 2.

[53]Ibid.

[54]Hersh, "Syria Calling," 10.

media, it was inconceivable to think that these pieces could have been published without the approval or consent of the Syrian regime. Especially in regards to Syrian relations with the United States, the regime was willing to influence public opinion to gain support for its policies. The regime did not wish to hear any alternative viewpoints that would challenge the regime's stance on this issue. In one of the notable pieces, Sami Moubayed, the editor-in-chief of *Forward* magazine, wrote of the benefits of improving relations, yet qualified his optimism with ten requirements that the Obama administration would have to meet in order to normalize relations. These were respectively: 1) the reinstatement of the U.S. ambassador to Syria and thus formal restoration of diplomatic relations; 2) the end of the U.S. government's anti-Syria rhetoric, which was very prominent during the Bush administration; 3) recognition by U.S. authorities of Syria's cooperation on the Iraqi border to stop the flow of foreign fighters and the insurgency; 4) U.S. cooperation to address the problem of the growing number of Iraqi refugees in Syria; 5) the abolition of sanctions and the Syria Accountability Act (E.O. 13338), and thus the normalization of economic relations between the two countries; 6) the facilitation of indirect Syrian-Israeli talks; 7) recognition of Syria's central role in resolving conflicts in the Middle East; 8) counterterrorism assistance; 9) an apology to the Syrian regime and compensation for the 2008 helicopter raid on the Abu Kamal village; and 10) the normalization of people-to-people diplomacy and distribution of visas to Syrian students who wish to study in the United States. Although it was a magazine article and did not cite or quote any Syrian foreign ministry official, many experts interpreted the stated conditions as those put forward by the Assad regime in order to launch a new era in bilateral relations. [55]

Despite the conditions that were circulated in the public, by which the Syrian regime tried to imply that the U.S. would benefit more from the reinstatement of relations than Damascus, Syria had much to gain

[55]Sami Moubayed, "Abu Hussein's Invitation to Damascus," *Asia Times*, November 7, 2008, http://www.atimes.com/atimes/Middle_East/JK07Ak02.html.

from building stronger lines of communication with the United States. For instance, according to U.S. officials, Assad's priority was to relieve Syria's economy from the sanctions. Because of that, from the very beginning, Obama aimed to change Syrian policies, and the potential easing of sanctions provided the administration with some leverage for discussions with Syrian officials —especially in high-tech industries, where the commercial aviation and information technology sectors were hit hard. These sanctions, which were crippling the Syrian economy, risked fomenting domestic instability in the context of the emerging global financial crisis and could threaten the Assad regime's survival.[56] Assad thought that easing relations with the U.S. and improving the country's economic conditions would strengthen his foothold in the country. The economic benefits were not the only expectation that Assad anticipated from the thawing of relations. He also wished to rescue his country from the international isolation it had faced in the aftermath of 9/11 and especially following the assassination of Rafiq al-Hariri by pursuing normalized relations with Western countries. U.S. officials interpreted this move as Assad's way of expanding his country's areas of diplomatic influence so as to include the United States. Political engagement in all forms, even photo opportunities, was highly emphasized over economic or security cooperation at the outset of communication.[57] In seeking interaction with the United States, Assad wished to project an image of international stature to both global and domestic audiences as a way to boost his legitimacy and popularity. This would also provide a significant degree of legitimacy for the Assad regime.

However, when the first steps of *détente* were initiated, both parties understood its nature quite differently. In 2008, Syria regarded its foreign policy with a sense of what one U.S. official called "triumphalism"; the country had survived its painful disentanglement from Lebanese politics after the Hariri assassination and also accrued great political capital in

[56]Interview by Kilic Kanat, July 2014.

[57]Interview by Kilic Kanat, July 2014.; See also Seymour, "Syria Calling."

the Arab world when it resisted the U.S. invasion of Iraq.[58] The country's warming relations with Turkey and France without apparent preconditions contributed to its pretension, making the Assad regime believe that it was negotiating with the United States from a position of strength. Most important, however, Syria endured the economic sanctions, heated regional politics and near-military clashes during the Bush era. Obama's 2008 campaign, which was based on his characterization as the "anti-Bush" candidate, provided hope to the international community and in particular Syria that his election would mark the end of the military adventures of U.S. foreign policy. During one round of the 2007 presidential debates, Obama promised that he would meet unconditionally with the leaders of the traditional pariah states in U.S. foreign policy, including Iran, Syria, Venezuela, North Korea and Cuba. In that debate, he argued that "the notion that somehow not talking to countries is punishment to them— which has been the guiding diplomatic principle of this administration— is ridiculous."[59] Thus, Obama's election was considered a victory for a new foreign policy approach of engagement as well as for Syria's hope of better bilateral relations.

Yet, while Syria was enjoying some form of triumphalism, U.S. State Department officials believed that it demonstrated hubris in its bargaining position with the United States. According to embassy officials in Damascus, such confidence reflected a naive understanding of the United States' political flexibility and intentions in its bilateral relationship with Syria.[60] Despite President Obama's willingness to launch a new initiative in regards to Syria, there were some significant political and technical impediments

---

[58]Interview by Kilic Kanat, July 2014.; See also Tabler, *In the Lion's Den*, 218; Alon Ben-Mei, "Above the Fray: Syria Reasserts it Centrality to Peace," *Jerusalem Post*, October 22, 2010, http://www.jpost.com/Opinion/Columnists/Above-the-Fray-Syria-reasserts-its-centrality-to-peace.

[59]"Fact Check: Would Obama meet 'unconditionally' with Iran?" *Political Ticker* (CNN blog), September 25, 2008, http://politicalticker.blogs.cnn.com/2008/09/25/fact-check-would-obama-meet-unconditionally-with-iran/.

[60]"Kerry - Assad: Improving the U.S.-Syria Relationship," WikiLeaks, WikiLeaks Cable 160, February 27, 2009, http://www.wikileaks.org/plusd/cables/09DAMASCUS160_a.html.

that would make such a quick rapprochement difficult. First of all, the full weight of Congress was against Syria at the time when Obama was pushing for warmer relations. Members of Congress were particularly reactive to Syria's support/ tolerance for foreign fighters flowing freely from Syria to Iraq, which contributed to the increasing number of American casualties in the war in Iraq. Secondly, despite the Obama administration's willingness to restore ties with a nation that could play an important role in the attainment of U.S. goals in the region, Obama's foreign policy was failing to increase the degree of engagement with Middle Eastern countries. There was a complete absence of a long-term strategy regarding relations with Syria, despite the fact that restoring ties with Damascus held tactical and operational significance for U.S. policy in the region. In fact, engagement with Syria at this critical juncture was crucial for the military disengagement from Iraq. Syria, in the final analysis, was peripheral to U.S. interests in the Middle East.

In addition, Congress certainly was not heartened by Syria's suspension of indirect talks with Israel in reaction to Operation Cast Lead against Gaza in 2008. Moreover, Syria's nuclear activity at al-Kibar put the administration in an awkward position regarding its non-proliferation priorities, as Syria refused to cooperate with the International Atomic Energy Agency's (IAEA) investigations. Therefore, if Assad proved uncooperative in his discussions with the United States, the administration would consider recommitting its resources elsewhere to achieve its regional goals.[61] That is not to say that U.S. officials did not value Syria; on the contrary, former Ambassador to Israel Martin Indyk described Syria as the linchpin for dealing with both Iran and Israel-Palestine. Former President Jimmy Carter's visit to Damascus in December 2008, just after the U.S. elections, also raised awareness in regards to the place of Syria in U.S. policy towards the Middle East and the future of bilateral relations between these two countries. Reportedly, the Syrian media's coverage of the visit was particularly impressive

[61]Interview by Kilic Kanat, July 2014.

and raised a lot of optimism about the prospects of bilateral relations, in addition to the return of the U.S. ambassador to Damascus, among the Syrian public.[62] During this period of transition, a group of Congressmen from the Armed Services Committee also visited Damascus and met with Bashar al-Assad. The main topic was again the future of relations between the U.S. and Syria. Assad shared his optimism during the meeting, with high expectations for the future of bilateral relations between the two countries.[63] However, despite these high-level visits and exchanges of opinion, the process was not an easy one for the Obama administration.

Efforts to repair ties and cooperate with Syria began almost immediately after Obama's inauguration in 2009, when he asked U.S. adversaries, including Syria, to "unclench their fists" and accept engagement with the United States.[64] This was in part the realization of the idea of restoring diplomatic ties and starting discussions with the rogue regimes of the international system. Though Secretary Clinton had centered her focus on the Asia Pacific upon indications that major policy issues in the Middle East would be addressed by the White House and Department of Defense, President Obama decided to utilize some resources of the State Department to engage with Syria and asked her to launch an initiative.[65] According to Andrew Tabler, President Obama imparted two guiding principles for engagement with Syria. First, it was necessary that the State Department pursue engagement with Syria in order to fulfill Obama's campaign promise to engage America's rivals. Second, warming relations were not in any way to threaten U.S. allies in Lebanon, who feared a Hezbollah

---

[62]"Special Media Reaction Report: Jimmy Carter's Visit to Damascus," WikiLeaks, Wikileaks Cable 886, December 16, 2008, https://wikileaks.org/cable/2008/12/08DAMASCUS886.html.

[63]"Codel Smith: Assad Positive on New Bilateral Relations," WikiLeaks, Wikileaks Cable 94, February 1, 2009, https://wikileaks.org/cable/2009/02/09DAMASCUS94.html.

[64]"Barack Obama's Inaugural Address," *The New York Times*, January 20, 2009, http://www.nytimes.com/2009/01/20/us/politics/20text-obama.html?pagewanted=all&_r=0.

[65]Michael R. Gordon and Mark Landler, "Backstage Glimpses of Clinton as Dogged Diplomat, Win or Lose," *The New York Time*, February 2, 2013, http://www.nytimes.com/2013/02/03/us/politics/in-behind-scene-blows-and-triumphs-sense-of-clinton-future.html?pagewanted=all.

victory in the June 2009 elections. Other than these stipulations, however, the State Department was given relative freedom to determine the terms of engagement.[66]

At the outset of rapprochement, the administration acted cohesively and cautiously, choosing to test the diplomatic waters in February 2009. As a gesture of goodwill to the Syrian government, the Department of Commerce allowed the country's national airliner, Syrian Air, to procure an export license for Boeing 747 spare parts.[67] The shortage of spare parts in the Syrian aviation industry was considered one of the most destructive dimensions of the economic sanctions. It not only risked passengers' lives and thus generated a confidence problem for a state-owned enterprise, but it also created a prestige problem for the Syrian government. As such, the end of these sanctions provided a huge relieve for the Syrian government. Shortly thereafter, Hillary Clinton exchanged a few words with Syrian Foreign Minister Walid Moallem in Egypt during a foreign ministerial meeting, arranging for future discussions between Syria and the U.S. that included Syrian Ambassador to the U.S. Imad Moustapha, National Security Council Middle East Director Daniel Shapiro and Acting Assistant Secretary of State for Near Eastern Affairs Jeffrey Feltman. At the very beginning, it was reported that Feltman's inclusion in the talks dampened Syria's enthusiasm for rapprochement. As the former U.S. ambassador to Beirut, he had made many enemies in Damascus for his sharp criticism of Syria's role in Lebanese politics, particularly after the Hariri assassination. Reportedly, in February's meeting, Feltman raised topics that antagonized Syrian officials, including Syria's support for Hamas and Hezbollah, interference in Lebanon, its nuclear weapons program and human rights issues.[68] Thus, Feltman's appointment and the February meeting made for a rocky start for warming relations.

[66]Tabler, *In the Lion's Den.*

[67]Sharp, "Syria: Background and U.S. Relations," 3.

[68]David Kenner, "Tough Love for Syria from Obama," *Passport* (Foreign Policy blog), March 3, 2009, http://blog.foreignpolicy.com/posts/2009/03/03/tough_love_for_syria.

Following the meeting in Washington, Clinton announced that Feltman and Shapiro would travel to Damascus in March to initiate talks with the regime. The initial steps of the rapprochement took place with the participation of different agencies from the U.S. government. During this process, Congress also played an active role in efforts to impact the direction of policy toward Syria. Senator Kerry, who had been a longtime supporter of diplomatic engagement with the Assad regime, paid a visit to Damascus shortly before the arrival of Feltman and Shapiro. He mostly laid the groundwork by visiting Assad on his home turf to discuss the parameters of engagement. After a conversation with the Syrian leader, Kerry expressed optimism about Assad's commitment to repairing Syria's relations with the West. According to Kerry, Assad seemed ready to change the course of his country and to politically engage with the Western world.[69] Senator Kerry's observations about Assad created a sense of hope among the pro-engagement officials in the United States. Feltman and Shapiro capitalized on these easing tensions by broaching a number of controversial topics, ranging from the stabilization of Lebanon and the revival of Middle East Peace talks to the containment of the civil war in Iraq.

The announced visit was, for many, an attempt to push Syria away from its partnership with Iran and a window of opportunity for Assad to reconnect with the Western world.[70] However, in every step of the process, the U.S. reminded the attentive public of the potential problems that they may encounter throughout the engagement. There was a high degree of skepticism among State Department officials in regards to the sincerity of Assad's steps. For instance, just before Feltman and Shapiro's visit, Secretary Clinton tried to temper the public's expectations for improvements in bilateral relations with Syria; nonetheless, policy analysts still considered the effort to be an announcement of a paradigmatic change in U.S. policy

[69]Kerry - Assad: Dividing Iraq and Unifying Iran," WikiLeaks Cable 158; "Kerry - Assad: Improving the U.S.-Syria Relationship," WikiLeaks Cable 160.

[70]David S. Cloud, "U.S. to Send Two Envoys to Syria," *Politico*, March 4, 2009, http://www.politico.com/news/stories/0309/19550.html.

towards the region and a great progress in engaging adversaries in the Middle East. Feltman and Shapiro were the highest-ranking administration officials to visit Syria since Deputy Secretary of State Richard Armitage's visit in 2005. Shortly after the announcement, they traveled to Damascus and conducted talks with Foreign Minister Walid Moallem, as well as presidential advisor Bouthaina Shaaban and Deputy Foreign Minister Faisal Miqdad. Officials from both countries publicly described the meetings as very constructive and said that they found "common ground" that would serve as the foundation for future improvements in bilateral relations.[71]

The developments that followed this meeting proved that meaningful steps had been taken to restore diplomatic ties and launch talks for cooperation in the region. For instance, upon the conclusion of the U.S. trip, Assad gave some interviews to international news networks. During these interviews, he announced that he was prepared to play a constructive role in the Middle East Peace Process. There were also some direct references to relations with the United States. In one of the interviews, he openly stated that he wanted to meet with Barack Obama in-person to discuss issues of mutual concern and interest. However, despite this public announcement, the administration believed that it was too early to provide Assad with such an opportunity to gain legitimacy.[72] Because of that, the Obama administration decided to continue talks with Syria at the current level through Shapiro and Feltman and wait for the regime to take significant steps before engaging in higher-level meetings. Nevertheless, the February 2009 trip to Damascus marked a clear break from Syria's political isolation witnessed in the Bush-era.[73]

Following the visit by Feltman and Shapiro, a delegation from the Senate and House of Representatives, led by Senator Benjamin Cardin, visited Damascus. During their visit, Bashar al-Assad received the members of

[71]Sharp, "Syria: Background and U.S. Relations," 3.

[72]Sharp, "Syria: Background and U.S. Relations," 3.

[73]Bilal Y. Saab, "On a New Footing: U.S.-Syria Relations," Brookings Institution, March 19, 2009, http://www.brookings.edu/research/articles/2009/03/19-syria-saab.

the delegation, who conveyed U.S. concerns. Several issues were tabled, including Iran's nuclear program, human rights abuses in Syria, the Israeli-Syrian peace negotiations, the elections in Lebanon and the issue of Syrian support for terrorist groups. A leaked cable from the U.S. Embassy in Damascus revealed the disagreement between the U.S. delegation and Bashar Assad in regards to these issues. According to the cable, Assad acknowledged that these are issues of serious concern for both countries; however, he requested that the delegation approach these issues from the Syrian perspective as well. For instance, Assad totally rejected the matter of Syria's support for foreign fighters. For him, Syria had nothing to gain from providing safe haven for foreign fighters and helping them organize attacks in Iraq. In addition, when Senator Cardin asked about the government's relationship with Hamas and Hezbollah, Assad responded by stating that both of these groups were elected representatives of the people in Gaza and Lebanon and that they were among the realities of regional politics. Assad also rejected the delegation's criticisms about human rights abuses in the country by arguing that Syria had made significant progress in human rights and that this point could not be discussed in the region while people in Gaza and Palestinian refugees were suffering under very harsh conditions.[74]

Jeffrey Feltman and Daniel Shapiro returned to Damascus in May 2009 to continue talks with the Syrian regime. Although observers interpreted Syria's warm reception of the visit as a positive step toward implementing the U.S.'s policy of engagement, the actual content of the talks was kept highly confidential. Speculation mounted that the talks addressed matters such as reinvigorating the Syrian-Israeli track of the Middle East peace efforts and engaging the country in matters of non-proliferation. Yet, some scholars, such as Syria expert Joshua Landis, were skeptical of these musings, arguing instead that President Obama sent Feltman and

---

[74]"President Assad and Codel Cardin Discuss a Nuclear Iran, Peace Process, Terrorism and Human Rights," WikiLeaks, Wikileaks Cable 179, March 10, 2009, https://wikileaks.org/cable/2009/03/09DAMASCUS179.html.

Shapiro to Damascus in order to signal the administration's resolve to the policy's strongest opponents, especially Israel. The visit's timing was key as, according to Landis, "[Obama] may want Israel to understand that it cannot make an end run around the President by going to Congress or the American Jewish community. During the week that AIPAC is meeting in Washington and senior Israeli statesmen are in town, Obama may simply be saying, 'I am in charge of U.S. foreign policy. I can engage Syria if and when I want.'"[75] Assuming Landis' premise was valid, Feltman and Shapiro's summer visit marked another major break from the Middle East policies of Obama's predecessor, which depended on unconditional support for Israel. It seemed that President Obama would follow a more nuanced approach in his vision of the Arab-Israeli conflict.

The geopolitical context of Feltman and Shapiro's May visit to Syria was quite different than that of their first. In that second meeting, U.S. officials met again with Walid Moallem in what they described as "constructive and comprehensive" meetings.[76] While handling this process, the Obama administration, on the other hand, was also trying to respond to concerns of those Syria-skeptics who argued that such a full-scale engagement could be considered a reward for Syria. Some observers of Middle East politics in Washington, DC frequently warned the administration of this idea. Following the expression of these concerns, in an interview with Al Jazeera, Feltman made it clear that "[Obama] believes that talking should not be considered a reward—talking should be the means to achieve objectives."[77] Publicly, Feltman purported that the visit marked progress but noted, "… this is part of a process and we'll see how it develops…I'm sure the Syrians will be looking at choices we will be making in the future, just as we'll be

[75]"What is Feltman Doing in Damascus," *Syria Comment* (blog), May 7, 2009, http://www.joshualandis.com/blog/what-is-feltman-doing-in-damascus/.

[76]Tabler, *In the Lion's Den.*

[77]"US Talks in Syria 'Constructive,'" *Al-Jazeera,* March 10, 2009, http://www.aljazeera.com/news/middleeast/2009/03/20093713536371310.html.

looking at choices that Syria is making."[78] These statements demonstrated a cautious optimism in regards to the future of rapprochement between the two countries.

Cables leaked shortly thereafter revealed the true nature of the discussions, which were apparently quite different than public pronouncements. According to the cables, Syrian officials conveyed profound disappointment in the way that the United States had approached the process of engagement. Syrian officials had made moderate concessions on Iraq and Lebanon, but they felt they had received little in return for their efforts. Walid Moallem expressed his skepticism about U.S commitment to repairing bilateral relations. Despite Syria's proximity to the Arab-Israeli conflict and its potential role, U.S. Special Envoy on Middle East Peace George Mitchell bypassed the country on his tour of the Middle East, instead choosing to go to more peripheral countries to the negotiations like Morocco.[79] More importantly, President Obama renewed the notorious *Syria Accountability Act*—which imposed strict sanctions for the country's state sponsorship of terrorism—just as Feltman and Shapiro left for their visit.[80] In a letter to Congress, Obama explained this decision to extend sanctions, stating that it was predicated on Syria's ongoing efforts to promote instability through terrorism, proliferation and insurgency in Iraq.[81] Nonetheless, the move jeopardized improvements in the U.S.-Syrian relations. Moallem followed up his criticism with a touch of hope that not all was lost, adding that he would consider moving forward in negotiations as long as the United States offered a tangible change in its level of commitment to

[78]"Teleconference by State's Feltman in Damascus, Syria," March 7, 2008 (online, IPP Digital, US Embassy), http://iipdigital.usembassy.gov/st/english/texttrans/2009/03/20090309124703eaifas9.014308e-03.html#axzz39x9r9Atm.

[79]"Feltman-Shapiro Meeting in Damascus: Israeli-Syrian Peace Issues," WikiLeaks, Wikileaks Cable 359, May 21, 2009, http://cables.mrkva.eu/cable.php?id=208124.

[80]"Feltman-Shapiro Meeting in Damascus: FM Muallim Questions US Commitment to Real Engagement," WikiLeaks, Wikileaks 335, May 12, 2009, http://cables.mrkva.eu/cable.php?id=206592.

[81]Laura Rozen, "Peace Envoy Mitchell to Damascus?" *The Cable* (Foreign Policy blog), June 3, 2009,http://thecable.foreignpolicy.com/posts/2009/06/03/peace_envoy_mitchell_to_damascus.

restore ties with Syria. Moallem suggested that as a show of good faith, the United States should signal to French, German and Spanish aerospace companies that they could export and service Airbus and Dassault planes without fear of U.S. reproach.[82] Yet, this concession was too much for the United States, which believed that offering the Syrian ambassador greater access to U.S. officials in Washington was concession enough without greater buy-in from the Syrian government.

A subsequent high-level meeting was arranged between Syrian and U.S. officials, this time in Washington, DC. Deputy Foreign Minister of Syria Faisal al-Miqdad was invited to the American capital to meet with U.S. State Department officials. This was the first high-level visit by Syrian officials to the U.S. in eight years. The negotiations on sanctions against Syria were the main point of order on the agenda. Little information was revealed pertaining to the content and outcome of these meetings. Foreign Minister of Syria Walid Moallem released a statement signaling optimism. He also mentioned the difficulties and problems of mutual trust in the process. He stated, "The agenda is clear; it is continuing the Syrian-U.S. dialogue to normalize bilateral relations. There are, of course, many obstacles and suspicions after an eight-year suspension of contacts. The gap must be bridged. We cannot expect or pin large hopes on a first meeting to accomplish this mission. This is a continuing process and this is part of the dialogue. Therefore, we view this step as important."[83]

Despite the problems and tensions during the meetings, the fact that the two countries began to engage in dialogue was considered a major step in the improvement of relations. Probably the most significant turning point in relations came in the form of a letter from President Obama to Bashar al-Assad in August 2009. Although the content of the letter was never made public, the letter demonstrated the commitment of the

[82]"Feltman-Shapiro Meeting in Damascus: Syria Wants Help with Civil Aviation Waivers," WikiLeaks, Wikileaks Cable 344, May 14, 2009, http://cables.mrkva.eu/cable.php?id=206978.

[83]Sharp, "Syria: Background and U.S. Relations," 5.

Obama administration to pursue its engagement with the regime in Syria.[84] After multiple high-level meetings, the priorities of the Obama administration became clear: bilateral relations would be improved on the grounds of Iraq, the Middle East Peace Process and nuclear non-proliferation. In this sense, the letter demonstrated the successful completion of this period and the introduction of full-scale engagement. Against this backdrop, an analysis of all three aspects of engagement is in order.

STABILITY IN IRAQ

Promoting both stability and security in Iraq was the main motivation for the Obama administration to reignite relations with Syria. The United States, anxious to withdraw its troops from Iraq, was frustrated with Syria's permissive attitude toward foreign fighters, allowing them to use Syria as a passage into areas under U.S. occupation. The White House recognized the need to co-opt Syrian support on this critical issue if it was going to deliver on the promises President Obama made during the presidential election. Therefore, Feltman and Shapiro pressured Syrian officials in May to stem the flow of foreign fighters into Iraq. They first named four fighters in particular known to be operating in Syria, requesting that the Syrian regime prevent their illegal activity. They next suggested that the Syrian government address the issue of foreign fighters more broadly. In both instances, the U.S. attempted to use carrots and sticks in order to persuade the Syrian regime to engage in more concrete steps regarding foreign fighters.

On the one hand, U.S. officials constantly reminded their Syrian counterparts that a stable Iraq would be beneficial not only for the Iraqi people, but also for Syria, which shares an important border with its neighbor. In particular, economic relations between the two countries could provide a win-win situation for the region and help raise economic prosperity within Syrian society. On the other hand, the U.S. warned the Syrian regime that

---

[84]Andrew Tabler, "Syria Clenches Its Fist," *Foreign Policy*, August 28, 2009, http://www.foreignpolicy.com/articles/2009/08/28/syria_clenches_its_fist.

an unstable Iraq had the potential to turn into an arena of sectarian insurgence, leading to the nation's disintegration into different factions. This scenario could seriously destabilize Syria as well. The Syrian regime, prior to the official meetings with members of the Obama administration, had emphasized the significance of the territorial integrity of Iraq for Syrian politics as well as Syrian relations with the United States. In one such meeting with Senator Kerry, Bashar al-Assad stated that the U.S. must ensure that Syria would not be fragmented into pieces. With the potential for such scenarios, political stability in Iraq was considered vital for Syria as well as the Syrian government.[85] Special Envoy Fred Hof stated that President Obama held very strong directives about securing the border between Syria and Iraq. Obama impressed upon Damascus—through his envoys, letter and messages—that any concession, such as easing of sanctions or increased trade would depend on Syrian cooperation on this matter.[86] During this period, cables from the U.S. Embassy in Damascus to Washington, DC demonstrated that State Department officials were closely watching the portrayal of the high-level visits from the U.S. in Syrian newspapers. The cables reveal that U.S. officials were particularly disturbed by the triumphalism emerging in the state-controlled media in the aftermath of the Congressional visit. One cable went so far as to suggest that U.S. officials should support the only private newspaper in Syria by providing talking points in order to amplify Washington's message for the Syrian public.[87]

In fact, the U.S. made it clear from the beginning that ending the transit of foreign fighters to Iraq would be the priority for the improvement of relations. Despite pressures, Moallem reportedly responded dubiously to these calls during the meeting. According to him, the matter was not an issue of political will but rather of the security capacity at the Syrian-Iraqi border. Moallem requested that the U.S. provide technical assistance and

[85]Ibid.

[86]Interview by Kilic Kanat, July 2014.

[87]"Re-engaging Syria: Entering the Syrian Spin," WikiLeaks, Wikileaks Cable 142, February 19, 2009, https://wikileaks.org/cable/2009/02/09DAMASCUS142.html.

military equipment, including night vision goggles for the Syrian military. There was some hesitancy among certain members of the State Department, which had been following Syria closely. According to embassy officials, the lack of military equipment was just an excuse for the Syrian regime. They asserted that the reality of Syrian support for the insurgency in Iraq was more complicated and providing military assistance was a wrong step to take. However, President Obama went forward and complied with some of the demands that are non-military and non-technical.[88]

Meanwhile, U.S. intelligence began taking concrete measures in an effort to prevent the flow of foreign fighters into Iraq through Syria by investigating source countries in different parts of the world to create effective cooperation. Through this cooperation, the U.S. would effectively block possible insurgents from these source countries before they would arrive in Damascus. This led to a dramatic decline in the number of foreign fighters sourced from Damascus. This situation, without much effort by the Syrian regime, decreased the tension between the two countries about insurgents in Iraq.[89] As such, the United States introduced a military element to the rapprochement by suggesting the institutionalization of a security program with Iraq to heighten the impregnability of the border.[90] To do so, U.S. officials offered to send a delegation from the U.S. Central Command (CENTCOM) to Damascus in order to discuss the potential for security cooperation.[91] With a little help from Senator Kerry to smooth rocky relations between the two countries, Hillary Clinton and Walid Moallem spoke over the phone in June to set a timetable for visits by the CENTCOM delegation and Envoy George Mitchell.[92]

---

[88]Interview by Kilic Kanat, July 2014.

[89]Ibid.

[90]"May 7 Feltman-Shapiro Meeting in Damascus: FM Muallim Questions US Commitment to Real Engagement," Wikileaks Cable 335.

[91]"May 7 Feltman-Shapiro Meeting In Damascus: FM Muallim Noncommittal On U.S.-Syrian-Iraqi Security Cooperation," Wikileaks, Wikileaks Cable 342, May 14, 2009, http://cables.mrkva.eu/cable.php?id=206976.

[92]David Ignatius, "Breakthrough with Syria, *Real Clear Politics,* June 3, 2009, http://www.realclearpolitics.com/articles/2009/06/03/breakthrough_with_syria_96789.html.

On June 12, 2009, the delegation from CENTCOM visited Damascus to discuss border security as well as attempts to stop the flow of foreign fighters. The possibility of specific mechanisms for joint efforts to sustain a peaceful border between Syria and Iraq was referred to during the meeting.[93] The CENTCOM delegation proposed a trilateral border monitoring group with Syria and Iraq to encourage burden-sharing and improve relations between the countries. The proposal included some specific mechanisms, such as joint assessments of several critical Syrian-Iraqi border crossings and the formation of a working group aimed at providing border security. The CENTCOM delegation also suggested that General Petraeus, who was invited by Bashar al-Assad to Syria, may visit Damascus if and once the relations moved in a desirable direction. However, during the first round of negotiations, Syrian analogues were especially concerned with the recognition of Syria's efforts on counterterrorism and the steps it undertook to secure its border with Iraq.[94]

A follow up meeting between the parties took place in August. The CENTCOM delegation, joined by high-ranking civilian officials, again proposed to begin a joint assessment of the border postings, providing a clear timetable for the task. Syrian officials agreed to discuss the matter but obstinately resisted yielding concessions, believing that they should be rewarded with a high-level diplomatic visit or the restoration of the U.S. ambassador merely for agreeing to the talks.[95] However, following the talks, the parties reached a tentative agreement to form a tripartite committee. Soon afterward, Nouri Al-Maliki of Iraq visited Damascus in order to seal the tripartite agreement for border security.[96] High expectations existed regarding Maliki's meeting with Assad, which had the

---

[93]"Border Security: U.S. Delegation Takes First Step with Sarg," WikiLeaks, Wikileaks Cable 426, June 21, 2009, http://cables.mrkva.eu/cable.php?id=213187.

[94]Ibid.

[95]"Codel Kaudman-President Assad Meeting May 28," WikiLeaks, Wikileaks Cable 337, May 29, 2009, http://wikileaks.ch/cable/2009/05/09DAMASCUS377.html.

[96]Tabler, "Syria Clenches Its Fist."

potential to facilitate a smooth execution of U.S. goals in Iraq. However, the debate proved moot as bad blood between Syria and Iraq ultimately poisoned the deal. Historically, Syrians distrusted Nouri al-Maliki, and Iraqis held contempt for Syria's support of exiled Baathists. Yet any hope of a security deal shattered when bombs exploded in Baghdad in August 2009, as Iraqi officials immediately accused the Syrian government of harboring those responsible for the attacks. Maliki demanded that Damascus surrender two ex-Baathists it withheld, and simultaneously implemented a strong border control to block the flow of fighters entering Iraq from Syria. Later, the crisis deepened when the Iraqi government broadcast a video of a confession of an al-Qaeda fighter who claimed to be trained by Syrian intelligence in Syria.[97] When the Syrian regime refused to extradite the two former Baathists without concrete evidence, Baghdad withdrew its ambassador from Damascus. This decision had an adverse impact on the relations between the two countries, and destabilized the tripartite arrangement that was agreed upon in August.[98] Several different explosions in Baghdad followed this episode, straining relations further. After another set of bombings on October 25 in Baghdad, new allegations emerged in regards to the role of the former Iraqi Baathists operating freely in Damascus. Although denied by the Syrian regime, the Iraqi Foreign Ministry as well as Iraqi embassy officials in Damascus stated that they witnessed the free movement of former regime elements in Syrian cities.[99]

By September 2009, the administration recognized that the trilateral discussions were dead in the water and looked eagerly for a viable alternative to demonstrate Washington's commitment to its relationship with

[97]Christopher M. Blanchard, Kenneth Katzman, Carol Migdalovitz and Jeremy Sharp, "Iraq: Regional Perspectives and U.S. Policy," *Congressional Research Services,* October 6, 2009, http://fas.org/sgp/crs/mideast/RL33793.pdf.

[98]Mona Yacoubian, "Syria and the New Iraq: Between Rivalry and Rapprochement in Iraq," in *Iraq, Its Neighbors, and the United States: Competition, Crisis, and Reordering of Power,* eds. Henry J. Barkey, Scott B. Lasensky, and Phebe Marr. (Washington, DC: United States Institute of Peace, 2011).

[99]"Iraqi Embassy Reports Worsening Syrian Iraqi Relations," WikiLeaks, Wikileaks Cable 820, November 24, 2009, https://wikileaks.org/cable/2009/11/09DAMASCUS820.html.

Syria beyond security cooperation, chiefly through water management, law enforcement reform and NGO development. The assumption held by U.S. officials was that Washington could entice Assad's government to better cooperate by engaging with it in areas of technical interest to boost "routine interaction." Conversations around "dangling" the prospect of fewer sanctions and greater public diplomatic engagement were also under consideration. In fact, six months after its first interaction with the Syrian government, the Obama administration began strategizing for the next six months. Preparation included diving into issues less related to military and security and more to the diplomatic-level of interactions. However, the plan also made it clear that the priorities of the administration and the foreign fighter dilemma remained at the top of the agenda. The Middle East Peace Process and the nuclear dossier came only after this significant issue for the United States.[100] As part of the continuation of diplomatic engagement, Deputy Foreign Minister of Syria Faysal Miqdad visited Washington, DC for meetings in September. This was the first time a Syrian envoy visited Washington in eight years. That said, the parties failed to reach a consensus about the steps needed for the first phase of negotiations between Syria and the United States.

MIDDLE EAST PEACE

The Syria-Israeli track of the peace process collapsed in 2000, and since then, the total abandonment of the process has prevailed, especially with the Second Intifada that year. Tensions between Tel Aviv and Damascus further increased when Israel targeted Palestinian units inside Syria in 2003 during the Ain es Saheb airstrikes. It was the first of such attacks inside Syria since the end of the October War in 1973. Meanwhile, U.S. support for the Israeli attacks also strained the already fragile relations between the U.S. and Syria. In the aftermath of the Israeli offense, President Bush justified the attacks as self-defense, stating that the United States can

---

[100]"Re-engaging Syria: Toward a Six-Month Plan," WikiLeaks, WikiLeaks Cable 671, September 10, 2009, http://www.dazzlepod.com/cable/09DAMASCUS671/?q=09damascus671.

resort to the same strategy to deal with potential threats in Syria.[101] These developments both damaged the prospects of Israeli-Syrian relations, specifically the peace process, and downplayed U.S. policy in the region.[102] This issue became increasingly peripheral to U.S. foreign policy.

During the Israel-Lebanon War in 2006, the crisis between Damascus and Tel Aviv reached a new peak. In several instances, Syrian officials signaled that Syria could enter the war on Hezbollah's side. They also allowed the Iranian government to provide supplies for Hezbollah forces using Syrian territory. Following this period, negotiations between Syria and Israel restarted with the mediation of Turkey. This was significant in two ways. On the one hand, it was considered the first major step towards the resolution of the problem since the Clinton administration attempted to mediate the dispute. On the other hand, the negotiations offered the potential to end Syria's isolation from the international community. According to some, the negotiations between Israeli Prime Minister Ehud Olmert and President Assad were not completely welcomed by the Bush administration. In fact, President Bush discouraged Olmert from resuming negotiations with Syria until the Assad regime implemented the steps outlined by the U.S. government. The Assad regime had signaled at different instances that it was willing to renew the negotiations under the mediation of the United States, but the Bush administration ignored the invitation. Despite Washington's opposition for the launching of this process, when the negotiations were announced in May 2008, the U.S. could not denounce or oppose it.[103] Nonetheless, this process could not reach its final goal of generating a long-term and sustainable peace between Syria and Israel because it was interrupted with the start of Operation Cast Lead by the Israeli Defense Forces in December 2008.

---

[101]International Crisis Group, "Engaging Syria? U.S. Constraints and Opportunities."

[102]Itamar Rabinovich, "Damascus, Jerusalem, and Washington: The Syrian-Israeli Relationship as a U.S. Policy Issue," Saban Center for Middle East Policy at the Brookings Institution, Analysis Paper no. 19 (March 2009).

[103]International Crisis Group, "Engaging Syria? U.S. Constraints and Opportunities."

The Obama administration perceived engagement with Syria as a way to reinvigorate the stalled Middle East Peace negotiations. The aftermath of the 2006 war between Hezbollah and Israel left the region incredibly unstable. Israel felt threatened after facing an unconventional challenge from a non-state group; Hezbollah was better equipped militarily and more politically involved in the region than the Lebanese state; and Iran began more aggressively pursuing its nuclear program. By courting Syria, U.S. and Israeli officials believed that they could diminish Assad's alliance with Iran and Hezbollah in an effort to blunt their influence.[104] Additionally, a renewed interest in the MEP Israel-Syria track would serve to demonstrate a strong U.S. resolve and improve U.S. credibility in other areas of involvement in the Middle East. President Obama gave the first sign of his intention to deal with this issue in his Cairo Speech in June 2009. Both his statements on the peace process and on the future of U.S.-Middle East relations signaled a new era for U.S. policy in the region.

Syria, both in its previous messages as well as during early contacts with the Obama administration, expressed its readiness to work with the United States on the MEP talks. In conversations with John Kerry in February 2009, Assad indicated a willingness to cooperate on the MEP initiative, calling the United States' stance on the matter "Syria's most important concern."[105] In the following days, Assad became more vocal about relations with Israel. For instance, he offered a "cold peace" to Israel and requested U.S. mediation in order to resolve the dispute between Syria and Israel. In these statements, he also suggested that a direct line of communication between Obama and himself would be more constructive in the resolution of several problems between the countries.[106] During a May

---

[104]Isabel Kershner, "Secret Israel-Syria Peace Talks Involved Golan Heights Exit," *The New York Times*, October 12, 2012, http://www.nytimes.com/2012/10/13/world/middleeast/secret-israel-syria-peace-talks-involved-golan-heights-exit.html?_r=0.

[105]"Senator Kerry: Syria Willing to Help Achieve Palestinian Unity," *Haaretz*, February 21, 2009, http://www.haaretz.com/news/senator-kerry-syria-willing-to-help-achieve-palestinian-unity-1.270630; See also "Kerry - Assad: Dividing Iraq and Unifying Iran," Wikileaks Cable 160.

[106]Tabler, *In the Lion's Den*, 222-223.

2009 U.S. congressional visit to Damascus, Assad made it clear that he was anxious to make peace with Israel: "If we don't achieve something now while Obama is President, it will be difficult in the future."[107] The Assad regime was eager to reclaim the Golan Heights in order to satisfy a decades-long political promise and boost domestic support. Though U.S. State Department officials questioned whether "the carrot of a Golan track will be an effective incentive" to encourage Syria to change other aspects of its foreign policy, the administration ultimately decided to push forward with negotiations in 2010.[108]

Though not observed as a priority, the Obama administration still placed the peace process on its foreign policy agenda. Although the more public and debated dimension of the process was the Palestinian-Israeli track, some members of the administration considered the Syrian-Israeli track to be an important prerequisite for the stability of the Middle East, which would render yet another U.S. intervention unnecessary. During the rapprochement with Syria, the Obama administration evaluated the possibility of a sustainable peace deal between Syria and Israel that would contribute to the stabilization of politics in the region. George Mitchell and Fred Hof made multiple trips to Damascus during this period. For the Syrian government, Mitchell's visit was particularly anticipated. The fact that he had skipped Damascus on his first Middle East tour had generated huge disappointment in Syria. After the meeting with Assad, Mitchell's tone echoed his position in past meetings with Syrian officials. He stated that reinstating negotiations between Syria and Israel was one of the near-term goals of the United States and that President Obama was determined to facilitate a comprehensive peace in the region. He also expressed that U.S.-Syrian relations were pivotal in providing ground for a more constructive role for the Syrian government in the region.[109]

[107]Codel Kaufman-President Assad Meeting May 28," Wikileaks Cable 377.

[108]"Kerry - Assad: Dividing Iraq and Unifying Iran," Wikileaks Cable 160.

[109]"Mitchel Cites Syria's Role in Mideast Peace Efforts," *The New York Times,* June 13, 2009, http://www.nytimes.com/2009/06/14/world/middleeast/14mitchell.html.

A month after this visit, on July 26 Mitchell made a subsequent trip to Damascus, holding a second round of talks with President Assad. After the meetings, Mitchell stated, once again, that both Syria and the U.S. are committed to providing a comprehensive peace that would contribute to stability and security in the region.[110] In fact, though Senator Mitchell did not illuminate which specific topics they debated, he claimed that the United States was "trying to develop...bilateral issues that we have with the Syrians" and noted, "[T]he United States is committed to a dialogue based on mutual interest and mutual respect and a solid foundation for discussion of our shared goals and of real differences, where they occur."[111] Purportedly, these shared goals included counterterrorism and stability in Iraq as well as progress in the peace process.[112]

During this period, a cable from Damascus to Washington, DC was leaked in regards to Turkish-Syrian relations. The document revealed that the U.S. was worried about the possible adverse effects of improved Syrian-Turkish relations on Washington's influence over Damascus as well as to an emerging peace process. It goes on to suggest that Turkish criticisms towards Israeli policies aid the Syrian government by emboldening the regime and eliminating the incentive for Syria to halt its relations with groups such as Hezbollah or to distance its position from Iran. Thus, increasing Turkish support for Syria was reducing the prospect for achieving peace in the region. According to the cable, "Turkey's methodical deepening of relations with Damascus offers Syria a strategic buffer against international pressure and a ready mediator willing to help Syria mend strained relations with neighbors... At the moment, the SARG is seeking to characterize Turkish-Israeli tensions as a show of Turkish solidarity with Syria and Palestinians."[113] The cable continues:

[110]"Obama's Middle East Envoy Steps Up Diplomatic Push in Syria."

[111]Ibid.

[112]"Kerry - Assad: Improving the U.S.-Syria Relationship," WikiLeaks Cable 160.

[113]"Turkish Support Emboldens Assad But Provides Best Hope for Coaxing Syria from Iran," Wikileaks, Wikileaks Cable 759, October 28, 2009, https://wikileaks.org/cable/2009/10/09DA-MASCUS759.html.

"While the US and Turkey generally share the same overriding objectives of regional comprehensive peace and stability, Turkish officials here stiffen when we broach the possibility of closer US-Turkish cooperation to influence Syria on specific issues (e.g., Iran or Lebanon). Given Ankara's jealous approach to Syria, one that applies equally to French and EU efforts to engage Damascus, our challenge is to nudge the deepening of Syrian-Turkish relations toward strategic Syrian choices necessary for achieving shared objectives, even if we differ with Ankara on tactical approaches."[114]

However, U.S. officials on Syria were also mentioned in the same cable as arguing that Turkey was the best hope for the U.S. to keep Syria away from Iran.

While the U.S. was planning to engage in peace negotiations and bring the parties to the table, there were several developments that generated a crisis in the region. One such event took place in November 2009, when the Israeli military allegedly seized a cargo ship in the Mediterranean Sea carrying nearly 600 tons of weapons from Iran bound for Hezbollah militants through Syria. This raid led to the mutual accusations on both sides. In a televised statement, Syrian Foreign Minister Muallem called the Israeli commandos conducting the raid pirates and denied that the ship was carrying weapons.[115] Efforts to contain the crisis followed in December 2009 in the form of a visit to Damascus by Fred Hof, the Special Coordinator for Regional Affairs. Hof met with Syrian FM Muallem who, despite the crisis, repeated Syria's willingness to engage in peace talks with Israel. According to a cable about the meeting, Muallem stated that U.S. involvement in direct negotiations launched with the facilitation of Turkey was a "practical necessity." However, in order for the U.S. to be considered an honest broker by the Syrian side, Muallem requested improvements in U.S.-Syrian bilateral relations. As a first step to reignite relations and as a sign of U.S. goodwill, Muallem proposed that the U.S. allow the Qatari government to transfer an Airbus 340 to Syria.[116]

[114]Ibid.

[115]Charles Levinson and Josh Mitnick, "Israeli Navy Seizes Weapons Believed to be for Hezbollah," *The Wall Street Journal*, November 5, 2009l, http://online.wsj.com/news/articles/SB125732536158927651.

[116]"Special Coordinator Hof's December 16 Meeting with FM Muallim," Wikileaks, Wikileaks Cable 868, https://wikileaks.org/cable/2009/12/09DAMASCUS868.html.

Later in 2010, Tel Aviv and Damascus entered a heated debate over the peace process, directing threats against one another. First, during a visit by the Spanish Foreign Minister, Assad told reporters that Israel is not serious about achieving peace, and that in fact, the policies of the Israeli government are pushing the region to war. Following this statement, Walid Moallem said that Israel should not test the determination of Syria and threatened to move the war to Israeli cities. Immediately after these statements, Israeli Foreign Minister Avigdor Lieberman warned the Syrian government that in any war with Israel, the Assad family would lose power. He claimed, "I think that our message must be clear to Assad. In the next war not only will you lose, you and your family will lose the regime. Neither will you remain in power, nor the Assad family."[117] Although these statements were common occurrences between the two countries, the fact that they came during a time when President Obama and the U.S. government were trying to mediate between the two countries created a major crisis not only between Syria and Israel, but also in U.S. relations with both nations.

From the fall of 2010 up until the spring of 2011, the White House tasked envoys Fred Hof and Dennis Ross with engaging in shuttle diplomacy between Damascus and Tel Aviv, which began at a time when the Palestinian peace track was at a standstill.[118] This process was kept very quiet throughout the interagency; outside the White House, only a handful of top State Department officials were kept apprised of the program's progress.[119] Discussions were largely predicated on Israel's withdrawal from the Golan Heights in exchange for a Syrian disengagement from Iran.[120] The meetings did not reach the finely detailed stage of determining the demarcation of the border, the timeline for Israeli troop withdrawal, and

[117]Isabel Kershner, "Israeli Minister Adds Heat to Exchange With Syria," *The New York Times*, February 4, 2010, http://www.nytimes.com/2010/02/05/world/middleeast/05mideast.html.

[118]Kershner, "Secret Israel-Syria Peace Talks Involved Golan Heights Exit."

[119]Interview by Kilic Kanat, July 2014.

[120]Kershner, "Secret Israel-Syria Peace Talks Involved Golan Heights Exit."

exact security arrangements.[121] Still, American officials indicated that negotiators were rapidly approaching an agreement. Reportedly, Ross told the administration that Syria was willing to limit its communication with Iran, Hezbollah and Hamas, give up its claims to the Sea of Galilee and work with the United States on counterterrorism issues. In return, Israel reportedly agreed to return the Golan Heights, cooperate on water issues and normalize relations with Syria by exchanging ambassadors immediately.[122] Officials entered the spring of 2011 quite optimistic about the status of the Israel-Syria track of the MEP negotiations.

NON-PROLIFERATION

Another dimension of U.S. policy towards Syria at the time entailed the issue of controlling weapons of mass destruction. This was a significant element of U.S. foreign policy both for its overall strategy on international security as well as its policy in the Middle East, in particular its relations with countries seen as contributing to proliferation. Even before becoming president, Obama outlined his vision of international security and politics in a commentary in *Foreign Affairs*, stating that the nuclear non-proliferation and elimination of weapons of mass destruction program was a significant part of his strategy. According to him, "America must lead a global effort to secure all nuclear weapons and material at vulnerable sites within four years—the most effective way to prevent terrorists from acquiring a bomb."[123] Later in his inauguration speech, his message to regimes about unclenching their fists was considered a message to Iran to terminate its nuclear program. Some elements of the U.S.'s rapprochement with Syria had to do with the Obama administration's decision to deal with nuclear

[121]Aluf Benn, "Assad's Israeli Friend," *Haaretz*, March 28, 2013, http://www.haaretz.com/opinion/assad-s-israeli-friend.premium-1.512146;

[122]Interview by Kilic Kanat, July 2014.; See also Tabler, *In the Lion's Den* and "Report: U.S. in secret talks with Syria over peace accord with Israel," *Haaretz*, January 1, 2011, http://www.haaretz.com/news/diplomacy-defense/report-u-s-in-secret-talks-with-syria-over-peace-accord-with-israel-1.334635.

[123]Barack Obama, "Renewing American Leadership," *Foreign Affairs* 86, No. 4 (July/August 2007), http://www.foreignaffairs.com/articles/62636/barack-obama/renewing-american-leadership

weapons. Solving the Syrian nuclear problem would be considered a first step and a test case to deal with the nuclear program of Iran. Those in the bureaucracy, who wanted the U.S. to fix its relations with Syria, also benefitted from this argument and considered the resolution of the nuclear issue a significant part of the package.

The nuclear issue and non-proliferation efforts were less public yet still important avenues for greater cooperation between the United States and Syria. The IAEA had been hounding Syria since the existence of the al-Kibar nuclear facility near Deir al-Zour became public information in 2007. Reports alleged that the government built the facility with help from North Korea in order to produce nuclear weapons. The facility was razed by Israeli airstrikes the same year, but IAEA tests in 2008, which Syria only begrudgingly allowed after it tried to conceal the evidence, still detected a high-level of chemically processed uranium in the soil. After this discovery in September 2008, the IAEA was prohibited from conducting any more investigations.[124] As such, Syria joined its ally Iran on the IAEA's blacklist, especially after the IAEA announced in 2011 that there was evidence Syria intended to produce weapons.[125]

The State Department believed that engaging Syria on a non-proliferation track might prove to be a promising facet of U.S.-Syrian cooperation. However, the impact of the Israeli strikes had generated an increasing degree of skepticism on the part of the Syrian government about any further cooperation with any Western country on the issue of its nuclear program. In order to overcome this impasse, the United States offered to conduct a "special inspection" of nuclear sites and assist Syria. The offer was not stated very vocally. In fact, the non-proliferation issue had never proved to be central to the bilateral relationship—that is, until Ambassador-Designate Robert Ford raised the concept in his controversial confirmation hearing in March 2010.[126] For those who took part in this process, what

---

[124]"Al-Kibar," *NTI*, December 6, 2013, http://www.nti.org/facilities/461/.

[125]Tabler, *In the Lion's Den*, 220.

[126]Tabler, *In the Lion's Den*, 240-241.

Ambassador Ford was trying to achieve was to find an alternative rationale for the restoration of ties with the Syrian government and hence, upgrade diplomatic relations between the two countries to an ambassadorial level.[127] During this process, some thought that the United States could encourage Syria to cooperate with the IAEA to abate the agency's onerous demands or else risk losing its recent warm reception from the international community. Others believed Syria might make moves on the Arab-Israeli process to distract the international community from the investigation.[128] Either way, increased engagement on non-proliferation would endorse Obama's stated foreign policy goal of non-proliferation, isolate Syria's ally Iran and act as a confidence-building measure between the United States and Syria.

In 2010, the State Department began its negotiations on this matter quietly, even among officials in the U.S. government. Bashar al-Assad initially rejected the notion of such engagement and warned diplomats not to put him "in (Iran's) nuclear basket *(sic)*."[129] He made that difficult for U.S. officials when he invited Iranian President Mahmoud Ahmadinejad and Hasan Nasrallah for a banquet to demonstrate that there was "no space between Syria and Iran."[130] Nevertheless, despite such public relations nightmares, those closest to Ford reported that he made great progress on the issue of non-proliferation, though details still lacked as to what such progress entailed.[131] Officials remained optimistic about negotiations with Syria in the months leading up to the Arab Spring.

Between 2010 and the outbreak of the Arab Spring, despite some setbacks, relations between Syria and the U.S. steadily improved. In February 2010, President Obama announced that Ambassador Robert Ford would be his choice for Ambassador to Syria. Following this, in the same

[127]Interview by Kilic Kanat, July 2014.

[128]Andrew Tabler, "How to React to a Reactor," *Foreign Affairs*, April 19, 2014, http://www.foreignaffairs.com/articles/66214/andrew-j-tabler/how-to-react-to-a-reactor.

[129]"Kerry - Assad: Improving the U.S.-Syria Relationship," Wikileaks Cable 160.

[130]Tabler, *In the Lion's Den*, 228-229.

[131]Interview by Kilic Kanat, July 2014.

month, Undersecretary of State William Burns met with Bashar al-Assad in Damascus and stated that it was a very useful meeting for both sides, demonstrating a level of enthusiasm for the future of bilateral relations.[132] More significantly, Syrian Intelligence Chief General Ali Mamlouk joined some of the meetings. According to a cable from the U.S. Embassy in Damascus, Mamlouk signaled that the U.S. and Syria could cooperate not only to provide border security between Iraq and Syria, but also to discover other potential aspects of a security partnership in different realms in the Middle East. During the meeting, he also reportedly suggested the necessity of cooperation between Syria and the U.S. on intelligence and security.[133] However, the Obama administration kept the details of the meetings confidential, avoiding any premature statements about the future of relations. During a hearing in the Senate, Secretary of State Hillary Clinton responded to a question about the prospects of relations with Syria with the list of several items, which constituted the backbone of the negotiations. She stated, "Just recently, Undersecretary Bill Burns had very intense, substantive talks in Damascus, and we have laid out for the Syrians the need for greater cooperation with respect to Iraq, the end to interference in Lebanon, and the transport or provision of weapons to Hezbollah, a resumption of the Israeli-Syrian track on the peace process, which had been proceeding through the offices of the Turks the last years, and generally, to begin to move away from the relationship with Iran, which is so deeply troubling to the region as well as to the United States. There are many specifics under each of those big-ticket items that we have discussed with the Syrians, and we are going to resume ambassadorial-level representation, but these issues have to be addressed continually."[134] Proba-

[132]Khaled Yacoub Oweise, "Syria's Assad holds security talks with U.S. official," *Reuters,* February 17, 2010, http://www.reuters.com/article/2010/02/17/us-syria-usa-burns-idUSTRE61G32Z20100217.

[133]"Syrian Intelligence Chief Attends CT Dialogue with S/CT Bejamin," Wikileaks, Wikileaks Cable 159, https://wikileaks.org/cable/2010/02/10DAMASCUS159.html.

[134]Hillary Rodham Clinton, Testimony before the Senate Appropriation Subcommittee on State, Foreign Operations, and Related Programs, *President's Proposed Budget Request for FY2011 for the Department of State and Foreign Operations,* Hearing, February 24, 2010, http://www.state. gov/secretary/20092013clinton/rm/2010/02/137227.htm.

bly among the most significant of these items was the reference to Iran and the U.S.'s willingness to keep Syria away from Iran. A day after this statement, during a meeting with Ahmadinejad, Assad declared that there was no distance between Iran and Syria, to the public dismay of Washington.[135]

The diplomatic thaw continued following these developments. In March 2010, a hearing was conducted at the Senate Foreign Relations Committee on the nomination of Robert Ford for Syria. During this meeting, Ford listed five main issues that would constitute the administration's agenda in Syria: 1) getting Syria to be helpful in stabilizing Iraq; 2) getting Syria to stop helping terrorist groups and to be more respectful of Lebanese sovereignty; 3) securing Syria's support for the peace process; 4) securing the Syrian government's cooperation with the IAEA; 5) encouraging greater respect for human rights in Syria.[136] It was an ambitious set of priorities and Ambassador Ford was cautious in responding to questions, avoiding raising expectations about the future of relations. During the hearing, Ford also underlined the significance of changing the relations between Syria and Iran. He stated, "While we and our friends in the region are working to mitigate Iran's influence, Syria has helped promote Iran's destabilizing policies...I do not think that the Syrians will change their policies quickly. Finding avenues of cooperation with Syria will be a step-by-step process that will require patience and steady commitment to our principles."[137] Following this, Senator Kerry, who was chairing the Senate Foreign Relations Committee during Ambassador Ford's hearing, visited Damascus to meet with Bashar al-Assad.

Amidst the diplomatic thaw, many serious tensions also surfaced as a direct result of Syria's actions. For instance, in April 2010, the Israeli government accused the Syrian regime of delivering SCUD missiles to Hez-

---

[135]Tabler, *In the Lion's Den*, 228-229.

[136]Senate Foreign Relations Committee, *Ambassador to Syria Nomination Hearing*, Hearing, March 16, 2010, Available online at: http://www.c-span.org/video/?292552-1/ambassador-syria-nomination-hearing.

[137]Ibid.

bollah. According to Israeli officials, these were accurate long-range missiles, which could put Israeli cities in grave danger. Although Syria strongly denied these accusations, Republican Senators in Congress signaled that they would delay the confirmation of Ambassador Ford if the SCUDS were really transferred from Syria to Hezbollah.[138] Following this, the State Department released a statement condemning any transfer of arms, especially ballistic missiles from Syria to Hezbollah. Soon after, Syrian officials were summoned by the State Department to request an explanation for concerns raised by the Israeli government.[139]

However, once again, the Obama administration continued the rapprochement with Syria. Shortly after the crisis over the SCUD missiles, Feltman attended a subsequent congressional hearing and highlighted the necessity of continuing to restoring diplomatic relations with Syria. Feltman claimed that rebuilding relations with Syria was particularly important to stabilize a region where U.S. men and women were actively serving. Feltman argued his country should utilize all assets at its disposal to convey messages about certain issues directly to the Syrian regime.[140] Shortly after, Secretary Clinton also clarified the necessity for the U.S. to continue diplomatic engagement with Syria. Clinton footnoted that this engagement was indeed not a form of reward for the Syrian regime.[141] Until the official appointment of the U.S. Ambassador to Damascus in January 2011, these diplomatic interactions continued between the two countries. Despite little improvement in these critical issue areas, the Obama administration opted for the continuation of rapprochement with Syria.

On the eve of the revolutions in the Middle East, Obama worked within his administration's centralized structure of decision-making while still

---

[138]Ethan Bronner, "Israel Says Syria Gave Missiles to Hezbollah," *The New York Times,* April 14, 2010, http://www.nytimes.com/2010/04/15/world/middleeast/15israel.html?adxnnl=1&adxnnlx=1416157255-Inhe9kK6dxNFqzUR+N37dA.

[139]Mark Landler, "U.S. Speaks to Syrian Envoy of Arms Worries," *The New York Times,* April 19, 2010, http://www.nytimes.com/2010/04/20/world/middleeast/20syria.html?_r=2&.

[140]Sharp, "Syria: Background and U.S. Relations," 8.

[141]Ibid.

engaging in a deliberative process with his cabinet and national security staff in order to craft U.S. policy on Syria.[142] Through this consultation, the administration was able to secure the endorsement of all key players in the government for diplomatic engagement. The only significant exception of this process was witnessed in the beginning of direct communication with Syrian officials. Some State Department officials were concerned about the possible perception of the U.S.'s attempt to mend ties with Damascus by the Syrian regime. According to them, the Syrian regime, from the outset, was cooperating just to gain some legitimacy and to relieve itself of the economic sanctions. They were also certain that the Syrian regime held a dishonest position concerning border security between Syria and Iraq. Moreover, they were convinced that the Syrian government would turn this rapprochement into a sort of a triumph and were skeptical about whether the Assad regime would fulfill its promises.[143] However, with the insistence of the officials at the higher echelons of the administration, they mostly acquiesced to the process. The avid involvement of the Secretary of State and her deputies, the National Security Council (NSC) and even the Senate, as represented by Kerry, demonstrated Obama's willingness to encourage the creative development of policy to achieve U.S. objectives.[144]

President Obama's Syria policy was tested with the emergence and rise of people's movements in different parts of the Arab world. After the revolutions in Egypt, Tunisia and Libya, and the spread of the wave of protests to Yemen and Bahrain, many analysts expected similar developments in Syria. The Assad regime began responding to these speculations very early on by suggesting that the Syrian political and social structures were fundamentally different from those of neighboring countries experiencing

---

[142]For more detail on President Obama's management style, see James Pfiffner, "Decision Making in the Obama White House," *Presidential Studies Quarterly* (June 2011), GMU School of Public Policy Research Paper No. 2011-13.

[143]Interview by Kilic Kanat, July 2014.

[144]David Ignatius, "Kerry's Unusual Role in Mediating U.S.-Syria Relations," *The Washington Post,* June 1, 2009, http://voices.washingtonpost.com/postpartisan/2009/06/_the_long-stalled_us_diplomati.html.

revolutions. In both national and international press, Assad stressed the difference between Syria and other states in the Middle East. During an interview with *The Wall Street Journal*, Assad stated,

> "We have more difficult circumstances than most of the Arab countries but in spite of that Syria is stable. Why? Because you have to be very closely linked to the beliefs of the people. This is the core issue. When there is divergence between your policy and the people's beliefs and interests, you will have this vacuum that creates disturbance. So people do not only live on interests; they also live on beliefs, especially in very ideological areas. Unless you understand the ideological aspect of the region, you cannot understand what is happening."[145]

Assad's optimism was also mirrored among the members of the U.S. government as the wave of protests were drawing near Syria.

---

[145]"Interview with Syrian President Bashar al-Assad," *The Wall Street Journal*, January 31, 2011, http://online.wsj.com/news/articles/SB10001424052748703833204576114712441122894.

THREE THE ARAB SPRING THUNDERS THROUGH SYRIA (MARCH 2011-AUGUST 2011)

❝ The U.S. administration began to think that it could no longer negotiate with Assad.

> "The Syrian people have shown their courage in demanding a transition to democracy. President Assad now has a choice: He can lead that transition, or get out of the way."[146]
>
> *President Obama, May 19, 2011*

The Arab Spring struck at an inopportune time for President Barack Obama, who intended to reorient U.S. foreign policy from the unstable Middle East to the burgeoning markets of the Asia Pacific.[147] Uprisings in the Arab world precluded Obama's ability to complete that pivot; however, it also pressured the United States to become more deeply invested in the turmoil economically and politically. By the time the Arab Spring struck Syria in March 2011, the bandwidth of the United States' foreign policy community was stretched thin across North Africa as uprisings arose in Tunisia, Egypt and Libya.[148] In February, the United States had called for its ally, Hosni Mubarak, to "stand down" in Egypt just days after turmoil struck and saw its call heeded when he was forced out of office by the military in mid-February. By mid-March, the United States had done the same for the Libyan leader, Muammar Gadhafi, and used force to back up that demand with the UN's endorsement and through NATO's intervention.

When uprisings broke out in Syria later that March, however, the Obama administration approached the situation with greater caution. It

[146]Barrack Obama: "Remarks by the President on the Middle East and North Africa," May 19, 2011 (online by The White House Office of the Press Secretary), http://www.whitehouse.gov/the-press-office/2011/05/19/remarks-president-middle-east-and-north-africa%20.

[147]Hillary Clinton, "America's Pacific Century," *Foreign Policy,* October 11, 2011, http://foreignpolicy.com/2011/10/11/americas-pacific-century/.

[148]Interview by Kilic Kanat, July 2014.

was possible to see this reluctance from Senator Kerry's approach after the first wave of protests hit Syria. Kerry, who was one of the point men of the Obama administration on Syria, tried to be optimistic about the course of the developments in Syria. In an address to the Carnegie Endowment for International Peace, he said that he still expected Assad to take steps towards political reform and move forward in its engagement with America and its allies. He stated, "My judgment is that Syria will move; Syria will change, as it embraces a legitimate relationship with the United States and the West and economic opportunity that comes with it and the participation that comes with it."[149]

The United States demonstrated restraint in responding to the protests in Syria for several reasons. Firstly, as for many other regional and global actors, Syria was expected to be less susceptible to the Arab Spring because of its social and political structure. After the peaceful transition of power from Hafiz al-Assad to Bashar, many analysts thought that al-Assad the son had completed the Assad's internal consolidation of power and had firm control over the country. Also, after the Hama massacres and decades of repression, many did not expect the opposition to organize and oppose such a consolidated and revolution-proof regime.[150] In addition, a well-organized opposition did not exist in Syria. In fact, many opposition groups were monitored by the extremely effective *mukhabarat* services.[151] Particularly, the State Department officials were skeptical about the capability of the opposition and some were even unwilling to engage these groups, which reminded them of the role that Ahmad Chalabi played before the invasion of Iraq. According to these officials, the meetings between U.S.

[149]Josh Rogin, "Kerry: It's Time to Give Up on Assad the Reformer," *The Cable* (Foreign Policy blog), May 10, 2011, http://thecable.foreignpolicy.com/posts/2011/05/10/kerry_it_s_time_to_give_up_on_assad_the_reformer.

[150]Stephanie Gaskell, "Interview with Ryan Crocker: Assad will Prevail 'Yard by Bloody Yard,'" *Defense One*, August 5, 2013, http://www.defenseone.com/threats/2013/08/ryan-crocker-id-go-syria-heartbeat/68132/.

[151]Emile Hokayem, *Syria's Uprising and the Fracturing of the Levant* (New York: The International Institute for Strategic Studies, 2013), 13.

diplomats and members of the Syrian opposition left more questions than answers.[152] Another reason for this hesitance was the lack of real-time information about incidents occurring in the country. The administration had trouble developing situational awareness on the ground as most U.S. embassy staff and contacts were concentrated in Damascus, far from the outbreak of the uprisings. According to some State Department officials, most of the information about Syria was received in Washington, DC instead of Damascus. During that period, information concerning incidents outside of Syria's capital often flowed from Washington to the U.S. Embassy in Damascus, and not the other way around.[153] For years, U.S. agencies demonstrated more interest in the strategic international dimension of Syrian affairs rather than the country's internal dynamics. As a result, American diplomats dedicated most of the spring and summer attempting to piece together stories from the news and personal reports in order to get an actionable understanding of events on the ground.

Furthermore, the administration had been making headway on the Middle East peace and non-proliferation talks. As such, officials shared a certain degree of hope that a settlement from Syria could be secured.[154] At the discrete request of these envoys, the White House held off on issuing too harsh of a condemnation of the regime for fear that it would jeopardize the possibility of negotiations, efforts for which continued until the summer. The State Department also overestimated the degree of the regime's political acumen and believed the government could absorb the blow of the uprisings if it chose to harness Assad's image to implement changes, which embarrassed the State Department after Hillary Clinton's extemporaneous comment about Assad as a "reformer" on *Face the Nation*. Questioned about Syria, Clinton underlined the differences between Libya and Syria, "Many of the members of the Congress of both parties, who have gone to Syria in recent months, have said they believe he is a reformer.

[152]Interview by Kilic Kanat, July 2014.

[153]Interview by Kilic Kanat, July 2014.

[154]Steven Heydeman, interview by Kilic Kanat, January 2015.

What's been happening there for the last few weeks is deeply concerning. But there is a difference between calling out an aircraft and indiscriminately bombing your own cities than police actions, which frankly have exceeded the use of force that anyone of us want to see."[155]

Instead, the regime proved more rigid, and hope faded after Assad delivered his defiant speech to the Syrian parliament in late March.[156] In fact, as stated by senior policymakers, the U.S. administration began to think that it could no longer negotiate with Assad.[157] Knee-deep in a NATO-mission in Libya that was turning out to be more complicated than expected, the administration then hesitated to make statements that could pull it more deeply into Syria. Moreover, the belief that regional actors, in the name of national interest, would choose to manage the crisis independently, precluding the need for extensive U.S. intervention, permeated the administration.[158] The United States also could not ignore the issue-linkage with Iran, with whom it did not want to imperil its nuclear negotiations.[159] Therefore, as U.S. interests were defined very narrowly in Syria in 2011, the administration failed to condemn Assad immediately the same way it had done with its ally Mubarak and enemy Gadhafi.[160]

Though aware of the political costs attached to direct involvement, the White House and the State Department were sympathetic to the democratic ambitions of the Syrian people. Barack Obama first criticized Assad for the violence at the start of April 2011. He made a statement condemning the Syrian government for the violence that it committed against the peaceful protesters. The administration, however, left a door open and outlined its expectations from the Syrian government as reform and an

[155]Lucy Madison, "Clinton: No Military Action in Syria for Now," *CBS News,* March 27, 2011, http://www.cbsnews.com/news/clinton-no-military-action-in-syria-for-now/;

[156]Interview by Kilic Kanat, July 2014.

[157]Interview by Kilic Kanat, July 2014.

[158]Interview by Kilic Kanat, July 2014.

[159]David Schenker, interview by Kilic Kanat, July 21, 2014.

[160]Interview by Kilic Kanat, July 2014.

end to the repression of its citizens. It was stated, "Until now, the Syrian government has not addressed the legitimate aspirations of the Syrian people. Violence and detention are not the answer to the grievances of the Syrian people. It is time for the Syrian government to stop repressing its citizens and to listen to the voices of the Syrian people calling for meaningful political and economic reforms."[161] Bashar Assad, however, did not respond positively to these calls and continued to target peaceful protesters throughout the country.

April 22nd of that year was to be remembered as the deadliest day in Syria, witnessing the death of 99 Syrians. Following the news, the White House released a statement condemning the violence. This time, the White House not only accused Assad of resorting to violence against his own people, but also pointed the finger at Iran for aiding the Syrian regime. The statement underlined, "President Assad is blaming outsiders while seeking Iranian assistance in repressing Syria's citizens through the same brutal tactics that have been used by his Iranian allies."[162] The statement called on President Assad to change course and respond to the demands of his people.[163] By April 29th, President Obama had signed Executive Order 13572, which declared the regime's "continuing escalation of violence against the people" a national emergency and instituted targeted sanctions. In his order, President Obama stated that the Syrian regime was responsible for committing "human rights abuses, including those related to the repression of the people in Syria, manifested most recently by the use of violence and torture against, and arbitrary arrests and detentions of, peaceful protestors."[164] The sanctions were not targeted at Bashar

[161]Barack Obama, "Statement from the President on the Violence in Syria," April 8, 2011 (online by The White House Office of the Press Secretary), http://www.whitehouse.gov/the-press-office/2011/04/08/statement-president-violence-syria.

[162]Kori Schulman, "A Statement by President Obama on Syria," *The White House Blog,* April 22, 2011, http://www.whitehouse.gov/blog/2011/04/22/statement-president-obama-syria.

[163]Ibid.

[164]"Obama Signs New Sanctions Against Syria," *The Huffington Post,* June 29, 2011, http://www.huffingtonpost.com/2011/04/29/obama-sanctions-syria_n_855593.html.

al-Assad, but rather some of his relatives and confidants. These individuals included Maher al-Assad, brother of Bashar al-Assad, Atif Najib, Bashar's cousin, and Ali Momlouk, the intelligence chief. In addition, the Obama administration sanctioned the Islamic Revolutionary Guard Corps-Quds Force, which was heretofore under UN sanctions for supporting different militant groups around the world. Through this order, the United States also revoked several licenses issued by the U.S. government in the past, granting the exportation of several goods and furnishings to Syria. Among them was a license issued for an airplane reserved for private use by Assad.[165] Following this statement, Hillary Clinton applauded the resolution put forth by the UN Human Rights Council in its Special Session on Syria, which condemned human rights abuses by the regime, calling on the establishment of an urgent investigation of the events.[166]

In May 2011, major figures from numerous government branches began to express their fading hopes regarding the Assad regime. Kerry admitted that he no longer viewed the Syrian government as willing to reform. He also mentioned that while Assad held an opportunity to reform in the past, this was no longer the case.[167] Disagreements throughout numerous government branches as well as partisan disputes over the Syria policy resurfaced following Assad's continued attacks on civilians. For instance, Senator John McCain claimed, "lawmakers' contention that Assad could be a reformer was one of the great delusionary views in recent foreign policy history."[168] For McCain, the miscalculation was not only that of Senator Kerry, "it was a whole lot of people, first of all the administration."[169] On the other hand, an equally important figure, Senate Intelligence Committee Chairwoman Dianne Feinstein, argued that Assad still had a chance

---

[165]Ibid.

[166]Hillary Rodham Clinton, "The Human Rights Council's Special Session on Syria," *Press Statement*, April 29, 2011, http://www.state.gov/secretary/20092013clinton/rm/2011/04/162260.htm.

[167]Rogin, "Kerry: It's Time to Give Up on Assad the Reformer."

[168]Ibid.

[169]Ibid.

to do the right thing. She asserted, "I don't think Syria has shaken out yet, I don't think we know what Assad will or won't do."[170] Meanwhile, in the proceeding Executive Order 13573, President Obama targeted senior Syrian government officials, including Bashar al-Assad, Faruk al-Shara and additional high-level authorities, mainly in response to the continuing escalation of violence by the Syrian government against the Syrian people.[171] However, one of the most significantly clear messages that the Obama administration conveyed to Assad originated from the President's speech on the Arab Spring in May 2011. Obama alluded to the gross human rights violations and attacks against peaceful protesters in Syria and emphasized that Assad still held a choice, "he can lead that transition, or get out of the way."[172] President Obama also stated that if the regime failed to cease its wrongdoings, "it will continue to be challenged from within and isolated abroad."[173] A significant dimension of this speech was in the link President Obama emphasized between the violence of the Syrian regime and its Iranian ally, stressing the way in which Tehran was assisting the Syrian regime with its tactics of suppression.

These statements and sanctions, in part, implied the end of U.S. efforts to restore ties with Syria. In this context, the United States began working at the multilateral level in June 2011, co-drafting a proposal with Canada that was later signed by 54 UN member states. The proposal essentially calls for the condemnation of violence and requests authorization for the creation of a UNHCR fact-finding mission.[174] Further statements from the U.S. government followed the proposal, conveying to the opposition

---

[170]Ibid.

[171]Executive Order 13573 of May 20, 2011, Blocking Property of Senior Officials of the Government of Syria, *Code of Federal Regulations*, title 3 (2011): 29143-29146, http://www.treasury. gov/resource-center/sanctions/Programs/Documents/13573.pdf.

[172]Josh Rogin, "Full Text of Obama's Middle East Speech," *The Cable* (Foreign Policy blog), May 19, 2011, http://thecable.foreignpolicy.com/posts/2011/05/19/full_text_of_obamas_middle_ east_speech.

[173]Ibid.

[174]"Fact Sheet on Syria," The White House, Office of the Press Secretary, August 18, 2011, http://www.whitehouse.gov/the-press-office/2011/08/18/fact-sheet-syria;

and many other actors in the region that the U.S. could potentially act in order to stop the violence in Syria. For instance, Secretary Clinton made a statement saying that the Assad regime is running out of time. She claimed, "They are either going to allow a serious political process, that will include peaceful protests take place throughout Syria and engage a productive dialogue with members of the opposition and civil society, or they are going to continue to see increasingly organized resistance."[175] Although there was an emphasis on an organized resistance, some members of the administration were already expressing views strongly against providing military aid to the opposition groups. According to them, any form of militarized civil conflict would bring radicalization, resulting in instability in Syria. The only way to prevent such radicalization was to form a moderate and unified opposition, but they were not very hopeful about the emergence of such an organization.[176] Later, this argument was frequently repeated in order to explain the position of inaction in Syria.

A critical development during this period was the visit of U.S. Ambassador Robert Ford to Hama as the crackdown on protesters escalated. The trip was not on the agenda and came as an individual initiative by Ford. He, along with the U.S. Defense Attaché, traveled to Hama with SUVs, and was surprisingly welcomed at regime imposed roadblocks by Syrian soldiers, who did not recognize the potential repercussions of such a visit. When Ambassador Ford reached Hama, the news of his visit spread in the streets. As people began to greet him, the gathering quickly transformed into a major demonstration.[177] According to reports, olive branch waving Syrians chanted on the streets, waving to the U.S. Ambassador's jeep; they placed red roses on the windshield and hood of his car.[178] Later, Ambassa-

---

[175]Hillary Rodham Clinton, "Remarks on Syria," July 1, 2011 (online by U.S. Department of State), http://www.state.gov/secretary/20092013clinton/rm/2011/07/167502.htm.

[176]Steven Heydemann, interview by Kilic Kanat, January 2015.

[177]Interview by Kilic Kanat, July 2014.

[178]Rania Abouzeid, "U.S. Diplomat Causes Firestorm with Visit to Rebellious Syrian City," *TIME,* July 8, 2011, http://content.time.com/time/world/article/0,8599,2082128,00.html.

dor Ford posted a message about the situation in Hama on his Facebook page, stating,

> The people in Hama have been demonstrating peacefully for weeks. Yes, there is a general strike, but what caused it? The government security measures that killed protesters in Hama. In addition, the government began arresting people at night and without any kind of judicial warrant. Assad had promised in his last speech that there would be no more arrests without judicial process. Families in Hama told me of repeated cases where this was not the reality. And I saw no signs of armed gangs anywhere – not at any of the civilian street barricades we passed.

Hama and the Syrian crisis is not about the U.S. at all. This is a crisis the Syrian people are in the process of solving.[179]

Ambassador Ford, while visiting the city, stopped at a hospital to visit those injured by the Syrian security forces and engaged in conversations with the protesters. This visit provided an important opportunity for the Obama administration to establish contact with the members of the opposition.[180]

The news of Ford's visit to both Hama and to the hospital made its way to Syrian government officials, who quickly condemned Ford's meeting with members of the Syrian opposition. Hama remains a symbolically important town for Syrian dissent. It is there where the father of Bashar massacred Syrian civilians in 1982. In its statement, the Syrian regime claimed that "the presence of the U.S. ambassador in Hama without previous permission is obvious proof of a clear evidence of the United States' involvement in current events in Syria and it is an attempt to incite an escalation in the situation which disturbs Syria's security and stability."[181] The U.S. State Department responded to the accusations by stating that the Embassy in Damascus had in fact practiced its due diligence by informing the Syrian Foreign Ministry of the visit. The State Department

---

[179]"A Note from Ambassador Robert Ford," Facebook post, July 10, 2011 at 7:10 a.m., https://www.facebook.com/note.php?note_id=10150237831306938.

[180]Hillary Clinton, *Hard Choices* (New York: Simon & Schuster, 2014).

[181]Martin Chulov, "Syria condemns US ambassador's 'provocative' visit to Hama," *The Guardian,* July 8, 2011, http://www.theguardian.com/world/2011/jul/08/syria-condemns-us-ambassador-visit-hama.

stressed that "the fundamental intention was to make absolutely clear with his [Robert Ford] physical presence that we stand with those Syrians who are expressing their right to speak for change."[182] The show of solidarity to the city by the top U.S. diplomat in the country energized and motivated the opposition, generating a significant degree of hope among the members of the opposition. Following this event, the escalation of the crisis continued with Syria's decision to restrict the movement of U.S. diplomats in Damascus. Shortly after that, the U.S. reciprocated the conditions imposed on them by Damascus and announced that from now on Syrian diplomats must also request permission prior to visiting Washington, DC.[183]

Following Ford's visit, relations between the two countries took on a growingly antagonistic tone. A few days after the Hama visit, the U.S. and French embassies in Damascus were attacked by pro-government mobs. Responding to this episode, Secretary Clinton stated that Assad had lost his legitimacy and should not observe himself as indispensable for Syria's future. She also claimed that the U.S. government had nothing invested in his hold on power.[184] In the following days, top State Department officials, including Clinton and Hof, met with what would become the Syrian National Council (SNC) to discuss the steps the U.S. could take to address the growing crisis. The members of the Syrian opposition made three requests for the United States in efforts to assist it: 1) a call for Assad to step down, 2) broader reaching sanctions, and 3) an effort to pass a UNSC resolution condemning the violence. The Obama administration accepted the three requests as the foundation of its plan, which was put into motion in August 2011.[185]

[182]Ibid.

[183]"Fact Sheet on Syria."

[184]"Clinton Says Syria's Assad 'Not Indispensable,'" *Voice of America*, July 10, 2011, http://www.voanews.com/content/clinton-says-syrias-assad-not-indispensable--125382213/142106.html.

[185]Radwan Ziadeh, interview by Kilic Kanat,

FOUR   OBAMA CALLS FOR
ASSAD'S REMOVAL
(AUGUST 2011-AUGUST 2012)

❝   While trying to avoid involvement,
the inner circle of the Obama White
House did want to give a message
to the world and to the Assad regime
about its position on the conflict.

> "We have consistently said that President Assad must lead a democratic transition or get out of the way. He has not led. For the sake of the Syrian people, the time has come for President Assad to step aside."[186]
>
> *President Obama, August 18, 2011*

The decision-making process in the U.S.'s denunciation of Assad was consistent with the general approach that Obama employed to address other issues during his time in office. Presidential theorist James Pfiffner characterizes Obama's approach as one that encourages deliberation but is highly centralized, featuring Obama as his own honest broker.[187] Other former members of President Obama's foreign policy team, including Vali Nasr, offer similar arguments in describing the foreign policy decision-making process at the White House and sometimes the exclusion of key personalities from debates and deliberations.[188] What made many observers of U.S. foreign policy in Syria frustrated with this process was a lack of policy, the absence of an interagency process and the constant emphasis on the message instead of strategizing policy responses for the crisis in Syria. Obviously, the Syrian conflict was something that the White House wanted to avoid to engaging in. However, while trying to avoid involvement, the inner circle of the Obama White House did want to give a message to the world and to the

[186]Barack Obama, "Statement by President Obama on the Situation in Syria," April 18, 2011 (online by The White House Office of the Press Secretary), http://www.whitehouse.gov/the-press-office/2011/08/18/statement-president-obama-situation-syria.

[187]Pfiffn Pfiffner, "Decision Making in the Obama White House."

[188]Vali Nasr, *The Dispensable Nation: American Foreign Policy in Retreat* (New York: Doubleday, 2013).

Assad regime about its position on the conflict. In most instances, the message seemed less costly and less risky and was seen as a responsibility-free way of dealing with complicated crises in different parts of the world. Many in the State Department consider this an unconventional way of formulating foreign policy and approached it skeptically.[189]

While trying to come up with a response in Syria, the Obama approach showed similar traits. According to some observers, the White House foreign policy team believed that Assad was going to lose power in a very short period of time. The President was right in his previous messages to Hosni Mubarak in Egypt. Rather than analyzing the differences and similarities between Egypt and Syria, some close advisors of President Obama were instead concerned that Assad may be overthrown before President Obama made any definite judgment about him publicly. Because of that, they pressured President Obama to make a statement about Assad without preparing any strategy that would make this message strong, determined and well-thought-out. There were also other expectations from such a message. According to many, not only would the rhetoric serve to position the administration on the "right side" of history in Syria, but it would also encourage military defections and empower the opposition to topple the regime without much investment from the United States, as it had done in Egypt. As David Remnick stated in his interview with President Obama, the President (as well as his inner circle) believed that his words could encourage positive change in different parts of the world. Such a message would create psychological support for the opposition in Syria and would simultaneously demoralize and isolate the regime. Moreover, it would improve the Obama administration's image worldwide by demonstrating its commitment to U.S. ideals.

According to Fred Hof, most policymakers in the administration agreed that the Assad regime was a "dead man walking,"—however, disagreement arose over "how long that walk would be."[190] Veterans in the interagen-

---

[189]Interview by Kilic Kanat, July 2014.

[190]Interview by Kilic Kanat, July 2014.

cy like Hillary Clinton and Leon Panetta believed that the recommen-
dation too greatly emphasized using messaging to shape public opinion
over crafting effective policy to bring down the regime. If Assad outstayed
the White House's expectations, they emphasized that President Obama
would have to back up his statement with action. Yet, Obama claimed in
the August 18 speech that the United States has "heard [activists'] strong
desire that there not be foreign intervention in their movement," relieving
the U.S. of any responsibility if and when the crisis worsened.[191] The NSC,
either confident enough in the power of rhetoric or so certain of Obama's
unwillingness to get involved militarily, did not advise the President to request contingency plans from the Pentagon. According to some, the White
House had not even consulted the military in high-level discussions until the end of 2011.[192] Therefore, members of Obama's NSC emphasized
rhetoric over policy in the decision to call on Assad to cede his role in
government. However, the repercussions of such a statement for the opposition and U.S. allies in the region extended beyond messaging; many of
them expected a corresponding strategy.

President Obama's statement on Syria constituted the first significant
split between the White House and the State Department. The Obama administration issued a statement on August 18 asserting that "Assad must step
aside," the supposed magic words that would mark the end of the regime.
President Obama stated, "The future of Syria must be determined by its
people, but President Bashar al-Assad is standing in their way. His calls for
dialogue and reform have rung hollow while he is imprisoning, torturing,
and slaughtering his own people. We have consistently said that President
Assad must lead a democratic transition or get out of the way. He has not
led. For the sake of the Syrian people, the time has come for President Assad

[191]Macon Phillips, "President Obama: 'The future of Syria must be determined by its people,
but President Bashar al-Assad is standing in their way,'" *The White House Blog*, August 18, 2011,
http://www.whitehouse.gov/blog/2011/08/18/president-obama-future-syria-must-be-deter-
mined-its-people-president-bashar-al-assad.

[192]Interview by Kilic Kanat, July 2014.

to step aside."[193] The statement was interpreted by the Syrian opposition, observers of U.S. politics and U.S. allies around the world as a commitment to overthrow the regime in Syria. However, many in the U.S. bureaucracy did not expect such a strong statement from the President. Accordingly, despite the public statement, neither the State Department nor the Pentagon had any plans or preparations on how to handle the situation. Moreover, according to State Department projections, Assad was not going anywhere in the short term. According to some, there were two significant issues that might complicate the calculations of President Obama's inner circle on the end of the Assad regime. First, the assumption was that the Asad regime would probably not commit major massacres of civilian protestors for fear of provoking an international military intervention of the type that was underway in Libya. And in the absence of massacres, the number of protestors would probably increase and the revolution would spread until the regime could no longer maintain control. This was the dilemma that would bring about Asad's downfall. Second, they underestimated the level of military assistance that the Syrian regime would receive from some countries in the region. Although the potential role of Iran was taken into consideration, some in the administration expected that, at a certain point, Assad would run out of ammunition. The foreign policy bureaucracy and other veteran officials were more skeptical about this projection. Lastly, for others, the administration was feeling the pressure of critical *Washington Post* editorials more than the pressure from allies and the Syrian opposition; the administration wanted to appease *The Washington Post*'s Editorial Board with a strong statement on Syria.[194] In multiple editorials in 2011, *The Washington Post* harshly criticized the Obama administration's inaction in Syria. In one of these editorials in April, the inaction was described as "shameless"[195] and in June, there was another editorial which stated:

[193]Obama, "Statement by President Obama on the Situation in Syria."

[194]Interview by Kilic Kanat, July 2014.

[195]"Shameful U.S. inaction on Syria's massacres," *The Washington Post*, April 22, 2011, http://www.washingtonpost.com/opinions/shameful-us-inaction-on-syrias-massacres/2011/04/22/AFROWsQE_story.html.

It seems fair to ask what Mr. Obama has done in response, given his pledge to employ all of the "tools" at the administration's disposal. The answer can be summed up in one word: nothing… The administration has excused its passivity by saying that it does not want to "get ahead" of allies in the region, and that it worries about the consequences of a regime collapse. But Mr. Assad's violence is already causing serious problems for Turkey and for Israel, which has twice faced incursions on its territory from Syria by Palestinian refugees organized by the regime. Other U.S. Arab allies are observing Mr. Obama's passivity with dismay: "Why doesn't the United States have a policy?" one senior official from the Persian Gulf recently asked us.

In fact, Mr. Obama enunciated a clear policy four weeks ago. He said the United States would use all its power to stop violent repression and promote democratic transition in countries such as Syria. He said his words "must be translated into concrete actions." But he has yet to act.[196]

Just before President Obama's "Assad must go" statement, *The Washington Post* published another editorial about U.S. inaction in Syria, in which they stated:

Until recently, the Obama administration was still describing the solution to Syria's crisis as negotiations between the regime and opposition. On Sunday President Obama, who has spoken in public about Syria only twice since the rebellion began in March, issued a statement saying he was "appalled" by the "horrifying" reports from Hama, "which demonstrate the true character of the Syrian regime." It was not clear, however, what action, if any, the administration was prepared to take.

Mr. Obama promised that "in the days ahead, the United States will continue to increase our pressure on the Syrian regime." But we have heard that before. On June 17, administration officials gave reporters a briefing in which they used those same words and talked about such measures as sanctions against Syria's oil and gas sector and the referral of Mr. Assad and his collaborators to the International Criminal Court on war crimes charges. Nothing has happened since then. Is it any wonder that Mr. Assad thinks he can slaughter the people of Hama with impunity?[197]

According to some, these editorials generated an intense debate within the NSC as well as the President's inner circle. They were considered critical ahead of a presidential race and added further pressure to provide

[196]"Silence on Syria," *The Washington Post*, June 15, 2011, http://www.washingtonpost.com/opinions/silence-on-syria/2011/06/15/AG9v0WWH_story.html.

[197]"Syria's Ramadan massacre," *The Washington Post*, August 1, 2011, http://www.washingtonpost.com/opinions/syrias-ramadan-massacre/2011/08/01/gIQAZHCKoI_story.html.

a message. However, many of the same members of the administration believed that, once stated by the President, this position would not constitute the main tenet of U.S. foreign policy. It became clear to all, shortly after the statement, that this was simply rhetoric preceding the strategy.[198]

The President's statement was accompanied by Executive Order 13582, issuing the harshest U.S. petroleum-related sanctions to-date on Syria. The order was fulfilling the first two items on the opposition's wish list. Obama then sought to fulfill the third request by approaching the UNSC to draft a resolution condemning the violence and urging a "Syrian-led political process."[199] The draft was presented to a vote in October 2011, but was rejected by China and Russia in the first double veto since 2008, causing U.S. Ambassador to the UN Susan Rice to storm out of the council.[200] Thus, the Syrian opposition's wish list was exhausted to little avail.

Even though some observers stopped expecting a diplomatic solution for the crisis in Syria following the attitude of Russia and China at the UNSC, the United States began to push for a multilateral approach to manage the conflict. There were several causes for the continuation of this diplomatic push. First of all, there were still serious domestic economic issues to be dealt with and under these circumstances a military solution for Syria, which would necessitate high-level U.S. involvement, was considered too costly. Secondly, American public opinion was reluctant to approve another "military adventure" in the Middle East and many in the Obama administration shared this view. In particular, the specter of American unilateralism in Iraq still haunted President Obama. After years of fruitless military occupation that only served to aggravate sectarianism in Iraq, the President had a strong aversion to any political or military

[198]Interview by Kilic Kanat, July 2014.

[199]"Russia and China veto draft Security Council resolution on Syria," *UN News Centre*, October 4, 2011, http://www.un.org/apps/news/story.asp?NewsID=39935#.U9XJ34BdVU4.

[200]Daniel Miller, "'They'd rather sell arms than stand with the Syrian people': U.S. envoy storms out after Russia and China veto U.N resolution," *Daily Mail*, October 5, 2011, http://www.dailymail.co.uk/news/article-2045442/US-envoy-Susan-Rice-storms-Russia-China-veto-UN-resolution.html.

action in Syria. For this reason, throughout the end of 2011, the administration only tried to take minimal symbolic steps by pronouncing statements against Assad. For instance, in October, the administration pulled out its ambassador from Damascus due to security concerns. However, the developments on the ground pressured the administration to take a more forceful stance. During this period, Vice President Joe Biden also generated debate when he claimed that the military intervention model that was used in Libya—coalition air power with rebel groups on the ground—could be utilized elsewhere.[201] Meanwhile, the American press was continuously reporting about bureaucratic infighting over U.S. policy on the Syrian crisis. For example, in one instance, there were apparent jurisdictional disagreements about sending emergency medical equipment to Syria. In this case, different agencies could not resolve their differences and no medical aid was sent. There were also reports of disagreements within the administration on how to approach the Arab League's monitoring mission. Some in the Obama administration were skeptical about the mission and argued that the bar for intervention was set too high in order to avoid any form of military intervention.[202]

In December 2011, media reports surfaced in regards to the increasing deliberation within the Obama administration on the many options available to assist the Syrian opposition. At that point, according to the UN High Commissioner for Human Rights,[203] the number of deaths by the regime had reached to 5,000. This number generated an increasing degree of pressure from members of the U.S. Congress, who believed that the

[201]Ewen MacAskill, "US pulls ambassador Robert Ford out of Syria over security concerns," *The Guardian*, October 24, 2011, http://www.theguardian.com/world/2011/oct/24/us-withdraws-ambassador-syria-robert-ford.

[202]Josh Rogin, "Obama administration secretly preparing options for aiding the Syrian opposition," *The Cable* (Foreign Policy blog), December 28, 2011, http://thecable.foreignpolicy.com/posts/2011/12/28/obama_administration_secretly_preparing_options_for_aiding_the_syrian_opposition.

[203]"Syria: 5,000 dead in violence, says UN human rights chief," *The Guardian*, December 12, 2011,http://www.theguardian.com/world/2011/dec/12/syria-5000-dead-violence-un.

Obama administration was too hesitant to stop the killings.[204] This report came after a statement by Fred Hof, concerning the possible fall of the Assad regime in the very near future, referring to the Assad regime as "dead man walking." Hof went so far as to request that the opposition prepare for the day that it took control of the Syrian state.[205] However, despite this growing criticism by members of the administration, the U.S. government continued to act slowly, failing to engage in a rapid response. Against the flood of criticism, the administration justified its position by stating that it needed to respond cautiously to avoid further destabilization in the region and to learn more about the complex nature of both Syria and the Syrian people. Reports suggest that the NSC started an informal and interagency process to collect options to provide assistance to the Syrian opposition. The process was led by the NSC Senior Director, Steve Simon. According to participating officials, this process "includes establishing a humanitarian corridor or safe zone for civilians in Syria along the Turkish border, extending humanitarian aid to the Syrian rebels, providing medical aid to Syrian clinics, engaging more with the external and internal opposition, forming an international contact group, or appointing a special coordinator for working with the Syrian opposition (as was done in Libya)."[206] According to the same reports, many members of the administration had already realized that the situation was not sustainable and recognized the fact that financial sanctions alone were not sufficient to bring about the end of the Syrian regime.[207]

The beginning of 2012 was again a period characterized by constant U.S. condemnation of the Syrian regime, but no meaningful action on the part of the Obama administration. In December 2011, the spokesman for

[204]Rogin, "Obama administration secretly preparing options for aiding the Syrian opposition."

[205]Matthew Lee, "US: Assad's Syria a 'dead man walking,'" *The Christian Science Monitor*, December 14, 2011, http://www.csmonitor.com/World/Latest-News-Wires/2011/1214/US-Assad-s-Syria-a-dead-man-walking.

[206]Rogin, "Obama administration secretly preparing options for aiding the Syrian opposition."

[207]Ibid.

the State Department stated that if the regime did not put an end to its policies, the international community might start looking for alternative means to protect civilians in Syria. Following this, in January 2012, Secretary of State Hillary Clinton condemned the regime's violent and brutal attacks against civilians in Syria and stated that if Assad remained in power, the instability might escalate and spill over the region.[208] In February, President Obama released a subsequent statement commemorating the 30th anniversary of the Hama Massacre and promised to help the Syrian people to achieve their goals. He also reiterated that the Assad regime must come to an end.[209] Some members of Congress became more critical of the administration's inaction and argued that the Obama White House must begin to consider alternative options to help the opposition within Syria. For the first time since the eruption of events, the possibility of arming rebels was openly discussed. According to a note released by Senators John McCain, Lindsey Graham and Joe Lieberman, the means of support had to include political and military assistance "to organize their activities, to care for the wounded and find safe haven, to communicate securely, to defend themselves, and to fight back against Assad's forces."[210] To achieve these goals, these three senators requested that the administration work together with U.S. allies in the region, including Turkey.

When the Friends of Syria meeting was launched in Tunis at the beginning of 2012, the members of the Obama administration provided more questions than answers about the situation in Syria. During the meetings, Secretary Clinton stated the necessity of a negotiated political solution to the crisis; however, later in an interview, she described the situation in

---

[208]Hillary Rodham Clinton, "Sharp Escalation of Regime Violence in Syria," Press Release, January 30, 2012 (online by U.S. Department of State), http://www.state.gov/secretary/20092013clinton/rm/2012/01/182720.htm.

[209]President Obama, "Statement by the President on Syria," Press Release, February 4, 2012 (online by The White House Office of the Press Secretary), http://www.whitehouse.gov/the-press-office/2012/02/04/statement-president-syria.

[210]"Graham, McCain, Lieberman Statement on Syria," Office of Sen. Lindsey Graham, Press Release, February 8, 2012, http://www.legistorm.com/stormfeed/view_rss/411052/member/44.html.

a more complicated manner. Secretary Clinton stated that the people in Aleppo must do something about the "illegitimate regime"[211] that kills innocent civilians and protesters. Her words gave the impression that the U.S. anticipated that if the residents of Aleppo joined the demonstrators, it would lead to the fall of the regime. To a question in regards to the possible threshold of violence that could trigger a military intervention in Syria, Clinton was murkier. She stated that there were many instances of violence in the world which were not well-documented or reported. Clinton argued, "it is important to stop and ask what that is and who's going to do it and how capable anybody is of doing it. And I like to get to the second, third and fourth order questions, and those are very difficult ones."[212] These statements created confusion among the observers of U.S. policy on Syria. In her memoirs, however, Clinton mentioned a discussion with the Saudi Foreign Minister, Prince Saud al-Faisal, about providing weapons to the rebel groups. The Saudi Minister stated that it would be an excellent idea to arm these groups and attempted to convince the Obama administration to follow suit on the plan. However, Clinton was wary about the further militarization of the conflict and feared the acceleration of the country's descent into a full-scale civil war.[213] From these messages, it was not clear what the Obama administration was planning to do about Syria. On the one hand, it sounded like the administration was expecting the fall of the regime once Aleppo joined the opposition, and on the other, it was trying to establish that a military intervention was a distant possibility.

The statements that came after Clinton's assertions were no less confusing. In a statement on Syria before the House Armed Services Committee, Secretary of Defense Leon Panetta made similar suggestions. After enumerating the Obama administration's endeavors in regards to Syria, he underlined the final objective of the administration by stating, "Make no

---

[211]Hillary Rodham Clinton, interview by Wyatt Andres, *CBS*, Sofitel Hotel, Rabat, Morocco, February 26, 2012, http://www.state.gov/secretary/20092013clinton/rm/2012/02/184662.htm.

[212]Ibid.

[213]Clinton, *Hard Choices*.

mistake—one way or another, this regime ultimately will meet its end."[214] Yet, he failed to provide a clear path to resolve the crisis, and instead resorted to comparing and contrasting the Syrian crisis with the Libyan conflict. According to Panetta, the operation in Libya was providing the Obama administration with lessons for the crisis in Syria. As in the Libyan case, the U.S. was following a multilateral and international engagement approach; it maintained regional support from the Arab world; offered substantial contributions; searched for a clear legal basis for the approach; and kept all options on the table, cautiously recognizing the limitations of the use of military force. In fact, it was not clear what the limitations of the use of military force were and if there were any conditions that would remove these limitations. Moreover, Panetta emphasized the lack of support from the Arab world and UNSC authorization for military intervention. He also suggested that, unlike the Libyan case, the opposition in Syria was not well organized. Despite these limitations, he suggested that they were "continuing to plan for a variety of possible scenarios should the President determine that further steps are necessary."[215] However, Panetta's presentation amounted to an additional set of conflicting and confusing statements by another member of the Obama administration. This intensified the scrutiny of the White House by outside observers over its Syria policy.

The 2012 national elections in the United States added another level of complication to the Syrian crisis. Obviously, the Obama administration did not want to take any risks over its policy in Syria, resorting to following a policy of diplomatic engagement on the one hand, and political and military avoidance on the other. In most instances, members of the administration indicated that sanctions against the regime were proving effective. Sanctions aside, the administration was less clear in terms of its direction on Syria.

---

[214]Leon E. Panetta, Statement on Syria before the House Armed Services Committee, "Secretary of Defense Testimony," Hearing, April 19, 2012, http://www.defense.gov/Speeches/Speech. aspx?SpeechID=1663.

[215]Ibid.

The elections added more ambiguity to this process. Foreign policy was not among the primary concerns of U.S. voters during this election and President Obama did not want the debate to shift to foreign policy in the presidential race. Thus, the administration worked through the UN and the Friends of Syria Group to address the political angle of the conflict. The UNSC was able to make progress by summer 2012, when it approved the ceasefire-monitoring group under Kofi Annan's six-point plan and issued the Geneva Communiqué calling for a transitional government in Syria. The Obama administration seemed to place an overwhelming amount of faith in this communiqué as a potential solution to the conflict. While the election was nearing, the administration believed that it had enough ammunition in terms of diplomatic endeavors and international engagement to respond any questions on Syria. Moreover, different members of the administration constantly emphasized the "war fatigue of Americans" and "low-level of support for a military intervention to Syria," and tried to pre-empt any criticisms from the Republican candidate on Syria. The administration believed that all of the possible politically-correct, risk-free and cost-free steps had already been taken to avoid any kind of damage during the elections: the strong message was given, the military intervention was avoided, the humanitarian assistance was provided, and diplomatic and multilateral endeavors were launched.

Throughout 2012, despite some multilateral attempts, the administration also began to refer to the Syrian problem as too intricate and complicated to deal with. Clinton referred to it as a "wicked one," one that defies standard solutions and approaches. According to her, every option was worse than the next. In her memoir, she explains the conflict and options in Syria by stating, "Do nothing, and a humanitarian disaster envelops the region. Intervene militarily, and risk opening Pandora's Box and wading into another quagmire, like Iraq. Send aid to the rebels and watch it end up in the hands of extremists. Continue with diplomacy, and run head-first into a Russian veto."[216] In 2012, the differences of opinion within the

---

[216]Clinton, *Hard Choices.*

administration about how to deal with the Syrian crisis also started to be seen more clearly. As Geneva efforts were halted, the Secretary of State and others within the administration searched for a solution that would include arming the moderate Syrian rebels. Clinton's plan depended on several motivations. On the one hand, arming a small group of moderate forces, regardless of its size, would give a big psychological boost to the Syrian opposition and pressure the Assad regime to agree to a political solution. On the other hand, such a move was necessary in order to stabilize problems with regional partners. In addition, such a well-trained and equipped force could also provide security and governance in the aftermath of the Assad regime, and prevent revenge attacks and chaos in the country. To achieve these goals, Clinton reportedly worked together with General Petraeus, who was director of the CIA by then, to set a plan to vet, train and equip moderate opposition fighters. The plan later received the support of Secretary of Defense Leon Panetta, who was equally frustrated with the deadlock in the region. Secretary Clinton also traveled to Turkey in August 2012 to discuss her plan, receiving feedback from Ankara. Two days after her visit, the Turkish Foreign Minister announced their agreement with her plan of action. Soon afterward, Secretary Clinton and Foreign Minister Davutoglu informed and discussed this issue with the foreign ministers of Great Britain, France and Germany.[217] Secretary Clinton presented her plan, supported now by her regional and European counterparts, to President Obama. According to Clinton, the plan also had a very high-level of support at the NSC.

However, the second group of decision-makers, including President Obama, considered inaction to be the best course of action and were unwilling to engage in any form of armed conflict in the region. According to Clinton, this second group included some of the top generals in the country.[218] It was later reported that those in President Obama's close ad-

[217]Ibid.
[218]Ibid.

visory circle at the White House were also skeptical about such a course of action by a president whose main election promise was to end U.S. military involvement in the Middle East.[219] Deputy National Security Advisor Ben Rhodes, who was considered to be a very significant member of the second group and a part of Obama's inner circle, later explained the reason for the decision. He claimed that "1) we wanted to make sure that we were providing assistance to people who we knew so that it wouldn't fall into the wrong hands given how many extremists were operating in the area" and "2) we didn't see a plan that was going to decisively tip the balance against Assad."[220] Despite some debate between these two groups, the decision of the President prevailed and the Obama administration continued to follow the same policy, failing to shift away from the policy of inaction.

Later in 2014, after Clinton published her memoirs and gave a set of interviews on the rise of ISIS and the situation in Syria and Iraq, this plan to arm the Syrian opposition had become a contested and controversial topic that created a major debate between the teams of Secretary Clinton and President Obama. It was revealed that, throughout 2011 and in most of 2012, the White House barred the State Department from engaging in any talks with moderate Syrian rebels. Reportedly, during this period and especially in mid-2012, the State Department cautioned the administration about radical groups and requested that the administration aid moderate forces so that they could emerge as the center of gravity on the ground. The State Department also warned the Obama administration that the conflict in Syria could potentially spill over to Iraq. Ambassador Ford, for instance, stated that the State Department warned the administration of the interaction between extremists in Iraq and Syria, and that Iraq and Syria could emerge as one all-encompassing conflict. However, the close inner circle at the White House, once again, preferred to stand

---

[219]Interview by Kilic Kanat, July 2014.

[220]Josh Rogin, "Obama Stifled Hillary's Syria Plans and Ignored Her Iraq Warnings for Years," *The Daily Beast*, August 14, 2014, http://www.thedailybeast.com/articles/2014/08/14/obama-stifled-hillary-s-syria-plans-and-ignored-her-iraq-warnings-for-years.html.

by its position.[221] Later, reportedly, the State Department prepared classified reports for the White House stating that "the Assad regime was much more durable than thought and was not on the verge of collapse."[222] The divide between the two groups prevailed after these reports. For Clinton, it was important to engage with the armed groups, as they were the only potential game-changer under the current circumstances in Syria. However, the White House continued to engage only with the non-armed civilian opposition groups. Despite some reports about the necessity to assist the Free Syrian Army (FSA), the Obama administration did not allow any agency to help the group in 2012.[223] The State Department even attempted to respond to the White House's concerns regarding the risks of arming rebels for U.S. security by trying to figure out who the rebels were and how to help them in a way that would not create any risk for U.S. security, but to no avail.[224]

In the meantime, the Pentagon was also evaluating its options in Syria. For the Defense Department, the primary concern was Assad's chemical weapons. According to the plans prepared by Pentagon staff, at least 75,000 troops were needed to enter the country and secure all of the weapons repositories. Considering the unacceptability of such a scenario, Secretary of Defense Panetta presented different and less costly options to the NSC, including the use of limited air attacks, protecting refugee camps and supporting regional allies.[225] In his memoirs, Panetta stated that there was not much support for any kind of military action among President Obama's top advisers. As a result, less aggressive measures such as coordinating a regional response and surveying Assad's air defense systems were evaluated. [226]

---

[221]Ibid.

[222]Ibid.

[223]Ibid

[224]Ibid

[225]Leon Panetta, *Worthy Fights: A Memoir of Leadership in War and Peace* (New York: Penguin Press, 2014), 370.

[226]Ibid.

During 2012, the Friends of Syria Group employed much of its early efforts to shape and strengthen the political opposition, out of a belief that a more legitimate political force could attract greater domestic and international support. The countries that participated in the group had also been members of the Friends of Libya, and as stated by Secretary of Defense Panetta, were willing to follow the Libya intervention model. Enthusiasm to participate in the Friends of Syria among members of the opposition was initially high because of the anticipation that they would receive military support, just as the Libyan opposition had. Yet, Hillary Clinton signaled the differences between Libya and Syria in January 2012, when she called Libya a "false analogy" for operations and instead pushed for a diplomatic solution.[227] Through the Friends of Syria, the United States pushed the SNC to more broadly represent Syria's various political beliefs, sectarian identities, genders and ethnicities, as a way to garner greater support inside and out of Syria. While the Syrian National Council, which became the Syrian National Coalition or Etilaf, became a more attractive interlocutor with the international community, it failed to have a strong resonance on the ground, as most of its members were trying to influence Syria from the outside. Therefore, the first initiative achieved modest gains but was not enough to shape the direction of the conflict.

The State Department also worked with allies and the opposition to develop a plan for a political transition after Assad's collapse. This was called "The Day After Project," which responded to many questions that were directed to the opposition about the nature of the regime and governance in Syria in the aftermath of the overthrow of the regime.[228] Yet, these efforts addressed a problem the opposition did not yet have; instead, the opposition needed a plan of action to unseat Assad in order to get to that

[227]Hillary Rodham Clinton, "Remarks at the United Nations Security Council Session on the Situation in Syria," January 31, 2012, http://www.state.gov/secretary/20092013clinton/rm/2012/01/182845.htm.

[228]"The Day After Project: Supporting a Democratic Transition in Syria," The Day After, August 2012, http://www.usip.org/the-day-after-project.

stage. Without the participation of the Pentagon or the CIA, such a plan would not be forthcoming and there was little the State Department could do to help. One State Department official familiar with the conflict criticized the administration's policy, claiming it focused too much on understanding the problem and not enough on solving it by unifying the armed opposition against Assad.[229] This initiative, while valuable, distracted U.S. resources and funding away from where it should have been focused.

Thus, the administration approached the first stage of the conflict in a very ad-hoc manner and throughout this period, there was some confusion and mixed messaging by and between the members of the administration. As August 2012 approached, it was quite clear that Syria would not experience an operation similar to the one in Libya. Though President Obama waited to call on Assad to step down at the request and advice of the interagency community, he heeded the advice of his core team of political advisors to make the decision to issue the August 2011 statement. There was very little consulting with various other agencies or departments during this period.

[229]Interview by Kilic Kanat, July 2014.

FIVE   OBAMA'S RED LINE
(AUGUST 2012-AUGUST 2013)

> " The red line speech was another
> demonstration of the White House's
> approach to foreign policy making: the
> message came before a strategy
> or a plan of action about what to do
> in case of a chemical weapons attack.

"We have been very clear to the Assad regime, but also to other players on the ground, that a red line for us is we start seeing a whole bunch of chemical weapons moving around or being utilized. That would change my calculus."[230]

President Obama, August 20, 2012

In August 2012, President Obama issued a statement that generated yet an additional turning point regarding the U.S.'s position on Syria. The statement arrived in the midst of mounting reports and concerns pertaining to the possible use of weapons of mass destruction by the Assad regime. A number of questions were raised among policymakers concerning the potential U.S. reaction in case of such an attack. Soon after, in response to these speculations, Obama stated, "We have been very clear to the Assad regime, but also to other players on the ground, that a red line for us is we start seeing a whole bunch of chemical weapons moving around or being utilized. That would change my calculus…That would change my equation…We're monitoring that situation very carefully. We have put together a range of contingency plans."[231] The language was not unprecedented, as the Armed Forces had been using the "red line" phrase in regard to chemical weapons in Syria since at least July, and Hillary Clinton used the phrase for the first time in a speech just nine days

[230]Claudette Roulo, "Little: Syrian Chemical Weapons Appear Secure," *Department of Defense News,* July 13, 2012, http://www.defense.gov/news/newsarticle.aspx?id=117118; See also "Hillary Clinton on Syria: use of chemical weapons is a red line – video," *The Guardian,* August 11, 2012, http://www.theguardian.com/world/video/2012/aug/11/hillary-clinton-syria-chemical-weapons-video.

[231]Ball, "Obama issues Syria a 'red line' warning on chemical weapons."

before Obama's statement.[232] During a press conference in Turkey, Clinton stated that the U.S. was working on the necessary contingency plans, including a response for the potential use of chemical weapons by the Syrian regime, which should be considered a "red line" for the world. Clinton also mentioned that they needed to plan for the possibility that these weapons would be used, specifically how to provide the necessary humanitarian and medical aid and how to contain those stocks.[233] As mentioned above, the Pentagon was already working on potential plans and scenarios to deal with chemical weapons.

Obama's statement, however, surprised the President's own administration, which had not been alerted to his position. According to members of the State Department, the administration had only begun communicating within the interagency and with U.S. allies about the likelihood and repercussions of a large-scale chemical weapons attack. Obama's public declaration of the U.S.'s position seemed premature and absent of further consultation.[234] Its introduction in the administration led U.S. policymakers to take the President's comment as a directive meant to reorient the focus of its policy in Syria to chemical weapons.[235] The move made sense given the lack of progress in other negotiations. The use of chemical weapons was considered a discrete, legal issue that would not require U.S. entanglement in Syrian affairs but had enough relation to Iranian non-proliferation negotiations to warrant the country's interest. Probably, the only exception to this situation took place a month before President Obama's statement, when a bomb exploded during a meeting of top-level security and mili-

---

[232]Claudette Roulo, "Little: Syrian Chemical Weapons Appear Secure," *Department of Defense News,* July 13, 2012, http://www.defense.gov/news/newsarticle.aspx?id=117118; See also "Hillary Clinton on Syria: use of chemical weapons is a red line – video," *The Guardian,* August 11, 2012, http://www.theguardian.com/world/video/2012/aug/11/hillary-clinton-syria-chemical-weapons-video.

[233]"Hillary Clinton Warns Assad 'Chemical Weapons Use will be Red Line,'" *YouTube,* August 11, 2012, http://www.youtube.com/watch?v=MdXckFEZkt4.

[234]Interview by Kilic Kanat, July 2014.

[235]Interview by Kilic Kanat, July 2014.

tary officials in the Syrian National Security Headquarters. Among those killed were senior security and military officials, including Defense Minister Dawoud Rajiha, Assef Shawkat—Deputy Defense Minister and the brother-in-law of Beshar Assad—and Hisham Ikhtiyar, the Director of National Security Bureau. The attack also wounded dozens, reportedly including the brother of Beshar Assad, Maher Assad, who also serves as the commander of the Republican Guards. Some in Washington were alarmed by this development, since nobody was expecting such a major blow from the opposition, which was considered too inept to conduct a military operation in Damascus. Those in the administration who favored a policy change considered the attack a possible game-changing blow to the regime in Damascus. However, there were no more subsequent attacks that could decapitate the regime and generate more defections from Damascus.

Following the red line speech, a statement was issued by the State Department in regards to the possible use of chemical weapons in Syria. It confirmed that Syria had stockpiles of chemical weapons composed of nerve agents and mustards gas.[236] Later in September 2012, Secretary of Defense Leon Panetta responded to questions on the use of chemical weapons by saying that the intelligence discovered limited movement of chemical weapons in Syria. According to him, most of the Syrian regime's chemical weapons were secured, although there were a few stockpiles unaccounted for. There was no information on the whereabouts of these chemical weapons stockpiles.[237] After these statements, allegations emerged in the international community about the use of chemical weapons in Syria. There were already several allegations by the Syrian opposition, which could not be confirmed by independent sources throughout the summer of 2012. In part, what made the administration react were these allegations

---

[236]"Timeline of Syrian Chemical Weapons Activity, 2012-2014," Arms Control Association, July 2014, http://www.armscontrol.org/factsheets/Timeline-of-Syrian-Chemical-Weapons-Activity.

[237]Lolita C. Baldor, "Syria Chemical Weapons Moved, Defense Secretary Leon Panetta Says," *The Huffington Post*, September 28, 2012, http://www.huffingtonpost.com/2012/09/28/syria-chemical-weapons-moved-panetta_n_1923159.html.

of the movement of chemical weapons by regime forces.[238] Following these unconfirmed reports, the first significant allegation of chemical weapons usgae by the Syrian regime was provided by the government of France in Salquin, near the border of Turkey in October 2012.[239]

According to observers of the Obama administration's Syria policy, the red line speech was another demonstration of the White House's approach to foreign policy making. Once again, the message came before a strategy or a plan of action about what to do in case of a chemical weapons attack. It is because of this that the administration had a hard time figuring out an action plan after each and every allegation of chemical weapon use and struggled to make a decision after the sarin gas attack in Ghoutta in August 2013. Later in several different speeches and statements, President Obama repeated his "red line" position. For the members of the admission, the message sounded enough like a deterrent and provided another cost and risk-free opportunity to stay out of the conflict in Syria, while also preventing the breach a significant international and humanitarian norm. Moreover, the statement was regarded as an assurance by U.S. allies in the region. Following this, however, some U.S. allies that had been imploring the U.S. for years to set a similar "red line" for the Iranian nuclear program expressed their disappointment for the lack of similar statements against Iran.

President Obama, starting with the August statement, made the chemical weapons issue an important talking point of his stance on Syria. In December 2012, President Obama reiterated his position in a speech at the National War College. He underlined all the positions that he endorsed since the beginning of the crisis in Syria and stated:

[238]"Syrian Rebels Claim Regime is Sending Chemical Arms to Borders," *NTI*, July 24, 2012, http://www.nti.org/gsn/article/syrian-rebels-claim-regime-sending-chemical-arms-borders/.

[239]"United Nations Mission to Investigate Allegations of the Use of Chemical Weapons in the Syrian Arab Republic," United Nations, September 13, 2013, https://unoda-web.s3.amazonaws.com/wp-content/uploads/2013/12/report.pdf.

"...Let me just say this. We will continue to support the legitimate aspirations of the Syrian people—engaging with the opposition, providing with
-- providing them with the humanitarian aid, and working for a transition to
a Syria that's free of the Assad regime. And today, I want to make it absolutely
clear to Assad and those under his command: The world is watching. The use
of chemical weapons is and would be totally unacceptable. And if you make
the tragic mistake of using these weapons, there where be consequences, and
you will be held accountable."[240]

Hillary Clinton just before her retirement made a similar comment in
response to a question on the potential use of chemical weapons by the
Assad regime. In Prague, she stated, "I am not going to telegraph in any
specifics what we would do in the event of credible evidence that the Assad
regime has resorted to using chemical weapons against their own people,
but suffice it to say we are certainly planning to take action if that eventu-
ality were to occur."[241]

The growing number of questions for U.S. officials on chemical weapons in Syria was a result of the increasing number of reports in the media
suggesting that the Syrian regime was, in fact, moving around its chemical
weapon stockpiles.

Issuing such a statement after Obama's electoral win in November held
significant repercussions for both the Syrian opposition and U.S. allies in
the region. Throughout 2012, the international community, because of the
U.S. Presidential Elections, did not expect much from the administration
in terms of Syria, but did anticipate a major move on this issue following
the elections. Although President Obama never signaled that there would
a policy change after the elections—and though he made some statements
hinting to his Syria policy during presidential debates—interested parties
on Syria never caught on. For example, during his foreign policy debate

[240]Barack Obama, "Remarks by the President at the Nunn-Lugar Cooperative Threat Reduction
Symposium," Press Release, December 3, 2012, (online by the White House Office of the Press Secretary), http://www.whitehouse.gov/the-press-office/2012/12/03/remarks-president-nunn-lugar-co-
operative-threat-reduction-symposium.

[241]Hillary Rodham Clinton, "Video Remarks on Syria," Remarks, December 3, 2012
(online by U.S. Department of State), http://www.state.gov/secretary/20092013clinton/
rm/2012/12/199997.htm.

with Romney, Obama argued that although he was committed to the idea that Assad must go, it would be hard for the U.S. to intervene in the conflict militarily. In regards to the arming of the rebels, he said that the U.S. needed to be extremely cautious on both who and how to arm. More importantly, little criticism or pressure was directed at Obama by the Republican presidential candidate, Mitt Romney, to suggest a more aggressive course of action in Syria. Romney also did not want to seem like yet another Republican presidential candidate in favor of using of unilateral military force to force regime change in another country in the Middle East. Because of that, both candidates avoided talking in length about the situation in Syria, despite the deterioration of the situation on the ground. The wishful thinking among regional allies and the Syrian opposition was based on the expectation that President Obama would impose a more assertive policy after the elections.[242] There were some news reports circulating, which emphasized that the White House made it clear that there would be no military assistance for Syrian groups until after the elections.[243]

There were other signs of the administration's increasing assertiveness. In the wake of elections, the U.S. made an important attempt to restructure the opposition and reorganize the coalition in a meeting in Doha, which was considered the boldest move of the administration since the beginning of the civil war in Syria.[244] When President Obama stated in late December that the U.S. formally recognized Syria's main opposition coalition as the legitimate representative of the Syrian people,[245] the hopes regarding a change in U.S. policy hiked dramatically. This announcement

[242]Sam Stein, "Mitt Romney, Obama Spar Over Syria," *The Huffington Post,* October 22, 2012, http://www.huffingtonpost.com/2012/10/22/romney-obama-syria-debate_n_2003918.html.

[243]Peter Foster, "US refuses to help Syrian rebels until after election," *The Telegraph,* July 16, 2012, http://www.telegraph.co.uk/news/worldnews/northamerica/usa/9404452/US-refuses-to-help-Syrian-rebels-until-after-election.html.

[244]Mike Giglio, "Post Election, Obama Gambles on Syrian Rebels," *The Daily Beast,* November 10, 2012, http://www.thedailybeast.com/articles/2012/11/10/post-election-obama-gambles-on-syrian-rebels.html.

[245]"US recognizes Syria opposition coalition says Obama," *BBC News,* December 12, 2012, http://www.bbc.com/news/world-middle-east-20690148.

came ahead of another Friends of Syria conference in Morocco, which the Syrian National Coalition attended for the first time. Against this backdrop, according to many opposition groups, there was little reason not to expect a more forceful push by the U.S. to end the conflict.[246]

In the period after his election for a second term, another major factor that influenced President Obama's foreign policy towards Syria was the September 2012 attack on the U.S. Embassy in Benghazi. The attack in Libya, the death of the U.S. ambassador to Benghazi and the ensuing fallout from the incident was a major contentious issue within U.S. domestic politics. Although not directly related to the conflict in Syria, the fact that the attack took place in a country where the U.S. was military involved in order to help the opposition resulted in a comparison between both cases. It was widely reported that the President Obama had been against involvement in Libya until certain members of his cabinet convinced the President to take action.[247] However, the outcome was far worse than expected. After what happened in Benghazi, President Obama's preference to avoid militarily involvement in the crises of the Middle East increased. In fact, after the specter of the Iraq War, the ghost of the Benghazi episode became another factor for President Obama's reluctance in Syria. The embassy attack, the murder of Ambassador Stevens, the controversy following the attack, the media scrutiny and the Congressional investigation generated a pool of complications for the Obama administration. After the Benghazi attack, those who were against military intervention attempted to accentuate commonalities between Libya and Syria, arguing that military intervention in Syria could not be an option.

In addition to the Libya attack, there was a major change in President Obama's foreign and national security team. Both Hillary Clinton, who prepared the plan to arm rebels in early 2012, and Leon Panetta, who supported Clinton's plan of action, left their offices. The new Secretary

---

[246]Mike Giglio, "How the U.S. Election Helps Syria," *The Daily Beast,* November 7, 2012, http://www.thedailybeast.com/articles/2012/11/07/how-the-u-s-election-helps-syria.html.

[247]Ryan Lizza, "The Consequentialist," *The New Yorker,* May 2, 2011, http://www.newyorker.com/magazine/2011/05/02/the-consequentialist.

of Defense, Chuck Hagel, was considered more cautious about the use of force. The administration's policy on Syria was mostly run by the new Secretary of State, John Kerry. Kerry, starting from his years in the Senate, had an interest in Syria and visited the country and met with Basher al-Assad on multiple occasions. Especially after the Obama administration's engagement with Syria in 2009, Kerry had visited Damascus in multiple occasions in a very short span of time. After the violent crackdown against demonstrators in Syria in early 2011, Kerry continued expressing hope about the possibility of Bashar al-Assad being a reformer until mid-2011. Now, two years after the beginning of the demonstrations in Syria, Kerry occupied the seat of Secretary of State and wanted to pursue an assertive foreign policy that would change the situation on the ground. He was particularly pro-active in trying to find a negotiating framework to bring together the opposition and the regime in his first month in office. However, these attempts did not generate a meaningful outcome that could change the conflict's equation. Besides, it was also revealed that, other than these diplomatic endeavors, U.S. foreign policy did not have a plan B to tackle the crisis and did not have any intention of becoming more involved in the conflict with riskier options.[248]

While the U.S. foreign policy team was being reorganized, there were different reports about the use of chemical weapons by the Syrian regime. First of these was a *Foreign Policy* report from a secret State Department cable that pointed to an indication of chemical weapons usage by the Syrian government in Homs. Both the State Department and the White House disputed the report.[249] Later, *Le Monde* released a more comprehensive report, where its reporters in Syria claimed to have individually witnessed, in several instances, the regime's chemical attacks near the outskirts of Damascus. Reporters saw the effects of several different attacks when the fighters of the FSA began displaying symptoms, such as shrinking pupils,

---

[248]Gayle Lemmon, "Kerry's Syrian Quagmire," *Foreign Policy,* May 31, 2013, http://foreign-policy.com/2013/05/31/kerrys-syrian-quagmire/.

[249]"US recognizes Syria opposition coalition says Obama."

blurring vision, breathing difficulties, vomiting and loss of consciousness. Among those exposed to the chemical weapons was, in fact, a *Le Monde* photographer in April 2013, leading him to suffer from blurred vision and respiratory problems for the next four days. The *Le Monde* report also indicated the increasing frequency of these types of chemical attacks by regime forces against the FSA. In particular, attacks took place in three areas of the Damascus region: Adra, Otaiba and Jobar.[250] There were differences in both the amount and the frequency of the use of gas in the respective areas, but there was no dispute that indeed all three localities witnessed gas attacks. Furthermore, the *Le Monde* report put forward an important warning in regards to the future of these chemical attacks: "The aim of the attacks seemed to be essentially tactical at this stage—an attempt to destabilize rebel units in areas where government soldiers have been unable to dislodge them, and at the same time a test. If Syrian army forces could dare to use chemical weapons in their own capital without setting off a serious international reaction, would that not be an invitation to pursue the experiment a bit further?"[251] The warning did not seem to generate any serious reaction in Western capitals. Later throughout spring 2013, new reports and allegations regarding the use of chemical agents emerged, this time occurring in other localities, including Idlib, Aleppo, Hama and Rif Dimashq. The UN mission was unable to verify these allegations, yet similar reports continued to mount throughout these months.

The first official U.S. announcement following allegations of chemical weapons usage came in April 2013, almost four months after the first reports of attacks. In a letter to Congress, the White House claimed, "the U.S. believes with some degree of varying confidence" that the Syrian regime used chemical weapons against its own people.[252] The White House's

[250]Jean-Philippe Rémy, "Chemical warfare in Syria," *Le Monde*, June 5, 2013, http://www.le-monde.fr/proche-orient/article/2013/05/27/chemical-war-in-syria_3417708_3218.html.

[251]Ibid.

[252]Kristen Welker, Jim Miklaszewski, Courtney Kube and Tracy Connor, "White House: US believes Syrian regime used chemical weapons," *NBC News*, April 25, 2013, http://usnews.nbcnews.com/_news/2013/04/25/17913974-white-house-us-believes-syrian-regime-used-chemical-weapons?lite.

statement was based on physiological samples. The administration asked the UN to probe the allegations. The statement also asserted, "We are continuing to do further work to establish a definitive judgment as to whether or not the red line has been crossed and to inform our decision-making about what we'll do next."[253] Both the Secretary of State and the Secretary of Defense confirmed the findings in a letter in the aftermath of the statement's release.[254] The letter was considered a significant development in U.S. policy towards Syria. In several instances, the countries in the region and the Syrian opposition alleged that chemical agents had been used by the Syrian regime. President Obama's "red line" speech was regarded as a serious commitment by the U.S. government to deter and—if used—punish the Syrian regime. The call by the U.S. for the UN to investigate the use of chemical weapons and its statements to further probe the allegations signaled a high-level of sensitivity, which might lead to a potential change in U.S. policy. However, at the same time, the administration's insistence on obtaining further evidence of the presence of chemical agents also reflected the inclination to avoid any intelligence failure that was witnessed during the Iraq War. Because of that, the administration was extremely cautious.[255] The political and diplomatic moves by the U.S. and the international community were perceived as sufficient on their own to deter Assad.[256]

The unanimous reaction to the allegations of the use of chemical weapons in Syria failed to bear any hint of consensus in statements by the various members of the administration. During the spring of 2013, different administration officials made multiple and sometimes confusing statements in speeches and in writing. In February, Leon Panetta, in his

[253]Ibid.

[254]Chuck Hagel, "Statement on Syria," Press Release, April 25, 2013 (online by U.S. Department of Defense), http://www.defense.gov/Speeches/Speech.aspx?SpeechID=1773.

[255]Michael Eisenstadt, "Investigating Alleged Chemical Weapons Use in Syria: Technical and Political Challenges," The Washington Institute, Policywatch 2072, April 26, 2013, http://www.washingtoninstitute.org/policy-analysis/view/investigating-alleged-chemical-weapons-use-in-syria-technical-and-political.

[256]John Kerry, "Press Availability on Syria," Remarks, February 28, 2013 (online by U.S. Department of State), http://www.state.gov/secretary/remarks/2013/02/205435.htm.

final appearance before Congress, answering a question about arming the Syrian rebels and a possible U.S. military intervention by mentioning the 2012 Clinton-Petraeus plan to arm the rebels. He claimed that he and General Dempsey both supported the plan. This statement was the first time that a member of the administration admitted endorsing a plan to arm the rebels in Syria.[257] Part of it was an endorsement to vet, arm and train moderate rebels in Syria affiliated with the FSA as a way to balance the growing al-Qaeda presence by instilling greater confidence among locals as well as the international community and attracting support. Overcome with a bad case of what Ambassador Hof called "Iraq Syndrome," which had only been exacerbated at this point by the NATO intervention in Libya, the President had no desire to engage militarily in Syria.[258]

President Obama's decision not to operationalize this plan revealed the growing interagency divide over Syria policy within the Obama administration. In a February 2013 congressional hearing, Senator John McCain said that he was disappointed that Obama "overruled the senior leaders of his own national security team, who were in unanimous agreement that America needs to take greater action to change the military balance of power in Syria," and that if there was "another time in history when a President's entire national-security team recommended a course of action and he overruled them...I'm not aware of it."[259] The statement of the outgoing Secretary of Defense once again generated a debate about the feasibility of this option. However, Obama's new foreign policy team was quick to point to the new direction. Secretary of State John Kerry explained that the best

[257] Jon Swaine, "Leon Panetta supports Hillary Clinton plan to arm Syrian rebels," *The Telegraph*, February 7, 2013, http://www.telegraph.co.uk/news/worldnews/middleeast/syria/9856382/Leon-Panetta-supports-Hillary-Clinton-plan-to-arm-Syrian-rebels.html.

[258] Frederic Hof, "Frederic Hof Criticizes Obama Administration's 'Iraq Syndrome,'" The Atlantic Council, August 22, 2013, http://www.atlanticcouncil.org/news/in-the-news/frederic-hof-quoted-in-the-economist.

[259] Michael Gordon and Mark Landler, "Senate Hearing Draws Out a Rift in U.S. Policy on Syria," *The New York Times*, February 7, 2013, http://www.nytimes.com/2013/02/08/us/politics/panetta-speaks-to-senate-panel-on-benghazi-attack.html?pagewanted=all; See also Dexter Filkins, "The Thin Red Line," *The New Yorker*, May 13, 2013, http://www.newyorker.com/magazine/2013/05/13/the-thin-red-line-2.

solution for Syria was a political one and that the U.S. was working towards this goal by trying to bring together another international conference that would include the warring parties.[260] Yet, shortly after this statement, the new Secretary of Defense, Chuck Hagel, claimed that all options were still on the table and that the U.S. could take different measures in order to deal with the conflict.[261] According to SNC representatives, it was mostly the Obama administration's inner circle that was not convinced by any option that other members of the administration brought forward. For them, there were clear indications that both Secretary Clinton and Secretary Kerry were sympathetic to arming the opposition and had seriously tried to convince the White House. However, the President did not want to initiate these plans at that time.[262]

Reportedly, Obama's opinion on lethal aid changed in June 2013, when the investigators found evidence of chemical attacks perpetrated by the regime. They were small in scale, but their very existence was apparently reason enough to cause the administration serious concern. Ben Rhodes declared in June, "The President has said that the use of chemical weapons would change his calculus, and it has."[263] The claim was true but incomplete. The use of chemical weapons justified U.S. efforts to give lethal aid to the rebels, but it was not because of the egregiousness of the attacks; senior State Department officials stated that the attacks at that point had failed to stir any grand response from the White House, save for inspiring further discussions to get allies to apply greater diplomatic pressure on Assad.[264] Instead, it appears more likely that the United States increased its support to demonstrate to its allies that it had "skin in the game," a

[260]John Kerry, "Press Availability on Syria," February 28, 2013.

[261]Lolita C. Baldor, "Hagel: US rethinking possibly arming rebels," *U.S. News,* May 2, 2013, http://www.usnews.com/news/politics/articles/2013/05/02/hagel-us-rethinking-possibly-arming-rebels.

[262]Radwan Ziadeh, interview by Kilic Kanat,

[263]Mark Mazzetti, Michael Gordon and Mark Landler, "U.S. Is Said to Plan to Send Weapons to Syrian Rebels," *The New York Times,* June 13, 2013, http://www.nytimes.com/2013/06/14/world/middleeast/syria-chemical-weapons.html?pagewanted=all

[264]Interview by Kilic Kanat, July 2014.

vested interest in the opposition's success. The United States' move to arm rebels came just as Saudi Arabia and Jordan excluded the U.S. from a rebel-training program out of a belief that it was holding reservations about the strength of its commitment.[265] Thus, military aid was wielded as a tool to propel political cooperation with U.S. allies going forward. In addition, this period also coincided with the increasing influence of Hezbollah and Iran in the Syrian conflict. For instance, Ben Rhodes, pointing to this increasing Iranian influence, stated, "There's urgency to the situation. There has been urgency to the situation for two years. It's particularly urgent right now in terms of the situation on the ground, in some respect, because we have seen Hezbollah and Iran increase their own involvement in the conflict, and that has caused an influx of additional fighters to the conflict. And so that has added an element of urgency."[266]

In a statement, Rhodes claimed that the intelligence community, according to the multiple and independent streams of information, assessed that the regime used chemical weapons multiple times in 2012. He also stated that "the United States and the international community have a number of other legal, financial, diplomatic and military responses available" and that the U.S. is prepared for all contingencies and will make decisions on its own timeline.[267] However, this announcement failed to end the dispute over the conflict in Syria among different members of the administration. Reportedly, immediately after the announcement, deep-seated divisions emerged within the administration over U.S. involvement. Secretary Kerry was among the proponents of

[265]Mazzetti, Gordon and Landler, "U.S. Is Said to Plan to Send Weapons to Syrian Rebels"; See also Adam Entous and Nour Malas, "U.S. Still Hasn't Armed Syrian Rebels," *The Wall Street Journal,* September 2, 2013, http://online.wsj.com/news/articles/SB10001424127887324202304579051280341316034.

[266]Josh Rogin, "Obama's Syria Aid: Too Late?" *The Daily Beast,* June 13, 2013, http://www.dailybeast.com/articles/2013/06/13/obama-s-syria-aid-too-late.html.

[267]Ben Rhodes, "Statement by Deputy National Security Advisor for Strategic Communications Ben Rhodes on Syrian Chemical Weapons Use," Press Release, June 13, 2013 (online by the White House Office of the Press Secretary), http://www.whitehouse.gov/the-press-office/2013/06/13/statement-deputy-national-security-advisor-strategic-communications-ben-.

more aggressive action, but Obama opposed putting American troops on the ground in Syria and the administration had not made any decisions on operating a no-fly zone.[268] In a leaked strategy meeting, Kerry and General Dempsey had a heated debate over possible operations in Syria. Kerry endorsed a plan that involved immediate U.S. airstrikes against Syrian airfields, specifically those that might be used for launching chemical weapons attacks against opposition forces. Dempsey, on the other hand, argued that such an operation would be too complex and that there was still no clear entrance or exit strategy or enough understanding of the consequences of such an action for the United States.[269] This division and lack of coordination was also reflected in bureaucratic circles. The administration failed to put together a structure, let alone a body, responsible for setting an agenda on Syria. An administration official told Gordon Lubold of *Foreign Policy* that he was quite saddened that after two and a half years, there was no sign of an effective, efficient and organized interagency task force.[270]

Adding to the disagreements over airstrikes within the administration, there was no coordination to operationalize military support or the arming of opposition groups. A CIA and special operations training program was put together for Syrian rebels on the use of anti-aircraft weaponry and encrypted communications program. The program was expected to expand in order to cover the training and arming rebels as well.[271] However, throughout the summer of 2013, little information was ever put forth on how to coordinate and plan the effort to arm the Syrian rebels. This interagency divide on arming the rebels was further reflected in news reports.

[268]Matthew Lee and Julie Pace, "Obama Authorizes Sending Weapons To Syrian Rebels," *The Huffington Post,* June 13, 2013, http://www.huffingtonpost.com/2013/06/13/obama-syrian-rebels_n_3438625.html.

[269]Jeffrey Goldberg, "Pentagon Shoots Down Kerry's Syria Airstrike Plan," *Bloomberg View,* June 18, 2013, http://www.bloombergview.com/articles/2013-06-18/pentagon-shoots-down-kerry-s-syria-airstrike-plan.

[270]Gordon Lubold, "Is Anyone In Charge Of U.S. Syria Policy?," June 20, 2013, http://foreignpolicy.com/2013/06/20/is-anyone-in-charge-of-u-s-syria-policy/.

[271]Lee and Julie Pace, "Obama Authorizes Sending Weapons To Syrian Rebels."

For instance, some anonymous sources from the administration stated that the new aid package would not include lethal arms, and limited only to military items that could increase the effectiveness of rebels on the ground. In the same report, a second administration official claimed that Obama might decide to provide lethal weapons to the Syrian opposition without informing large parts of the national security bureaucracy due to its secret nature.[272] A third administration official—senior this time—explained the nature of the assistance to the Syrian opposition as symbolic. According to him, the announcement had the potential to shift "the emotional balance by giving the rebels hope and making Syrian President Bashar al-Assad fear that his opposition will become a more formidable force."[273]

Yet, the United States was not timely in delivering that aid, delaying much of it until the spring of 2014. The setback cast doubts over the sincerity of the proposal and contributed to the declining of U.S. credibility among the Syrian opposition. It also added to the deterioration of relations with regional partners. Even when the aid was delivered, it did little to change the balance of power on the ground. Critics and administration officials alike asserted that this push was ineffective by design, as Al-Qaeda-related groups were getting stronger and the political opposition was incapable of leading. For a group of people in Washington, Assad was arguably the only source of stability capable of preventing the state institutions from crumbling. They believed that Assad was the only chance to avoid the collapse of the country into a safe haven for terrorist groups. According to senior military officers, the Pentagon was expressly told not to draft military strike options that would facilitate Assad's ousting, as it would leave a power vacuum in the country.[274] Even Dempsey repeatedly approached Congress to iterate his concern that Assad's removal from

[272]Rogin, "Obama's Syria Aid: Too Late?"

[273]James Traub, "Terms Of Engagement: Is Doing Something in Syria Better than Nothing?," *Foreign Policy,* June 14, 2013, http://foreignpolicy.com/2013/06/14/is-doing-something-in-syria-better-than-nothing/.

[274]Entous and Malas, "U.S. Still Hasn't Armed Syrian Rebels."

power would inevitably strengthen al-Qaeda and its affiliates.[275] Therefore, the United States deliberately failed to pick the opposition as the winner, allowing for the development of a war of attrition in Syria, while simultaneously fostering an atmosphere of impunity for the Assad regime. In making his decision on whether to arm the opposition, President Obama made a unilateral decision, isolating himself inside his own administration.

[275]Ibid.

SIX   A NEW CALCULUS
(AUGUST 2013-AUGUST 2014)

❝ Some U.S. allies in the region
as well as many members of the
Syrian opposition saw the shift as
an effort to backpedal on the plan,
either to deflect blame in the event of
failure or to use the polarized Congress
to prevent its approval all together.

"Now, after careful deliberation, I have decided that the United States should take military action against Syrian regime targets...I will seek authorization for the use of force from the American people's representatives in Congress."[276]

President Obama, August 31, 2013

On August 21, 2013, President Obama's "red line" statement was challenged in the largest incident of chemical weapons use in the conflict to-date, killing up to an estimated 1,400 people in the Damascus suburb of Ghouta. A few other chemical attacks were reported in November 2012 and March and April 2013, but this latest attack was both the largest and the most well reported one. In addition to the high number of casualties, the aftermath of the attacks and the affected patients' conditions were recorded and distributed through social media. The news of the attack was quickly circulated throughout the world in a very short period of time. The attack in Ghouta was impossible to ignore and warranted the involvement of the White House. It was a shocking incident for the Obama administration because many in the White House believed that the red line speech would constitute a major deterrent against the Syrian regime's use of chemical weapons. Furthermore, ever since the red line statement, the Obama administration had sent messages for both Iran and Russia explaining the possible consequences of the use of these weapons.[277]

[276]Barack Obama, "Statement by the President on Syria," Press Release, August 31, 2013 (online by the White House Office of the Press Secretary), http://www.whitehouse.gov/the-press-office/2013/08/31/statement-president-syria.

[277]Peter Baker, Mark Landler, David Sanger and Anne Barnard, "Off-the-Cuff Obama Line Put U.S. in Bind on Syria," *The New York Times,* May 4, 2013, http://www.nytimes.com/2013/05/05/world/middleeast/obamas-vow-on-chemical-weapons-puts-him-in-tough-spot.html?pagewanted=all&_r=0 .

Although there were previous intelligence reports about the use of these weapons, the time between the attacks and the confirmation of the use of chemical agents was such that the issue was no longer on the agenda. In addition, in previous attacks, finding conclusive evidence about the use of chemical weapons was difficult. According to rebel forces, in one particular instance, after a chemical weapons attack by Syrian regime forces, "American intelligence officers in Jordan were provided two sets of hair, soil and urine samples from each of three contested areas near Damascus where rebels have accused the government of using chemical weapons. After positive tests… the officers asked for a third sample, but it could not be delivered along an impassable road."[278] The attack in Ghouta, however, was much different than previous instances. In particular, the YouTube videos that were circulated on social media in the immediate aftermath of the attack demonstrated that the victims were suffering from exposure to a chemical agent, including difficulty breathing, convulsion and foaming of the mouth. According to experts, this kind of initial visual evidence showed the use of chemical weapons.[279]

Now all the eyes again turned to the United States and President Obama, who had made a statement about the chemical attacks exactly one year ago. According to many, if it was also substantiated by intelligence reports, this was a clear violation of the red line set forth by the President himself and necessitated a swift U.S. response. First, the attack was a grave violation of international chemical weapons bans and international norms. As the global superpower, the United States, with backing from the international community, needed to act in order to sanction those who used these weapons. Second, the attack cast a shadow over the Iranian nuclear negotiations, which President Obama had been pushing as a foreign policy priority. If the United States failed to follow through on its 2012

[278]Ibid.

[279]Dashiell Bennett, "The Visual Evidence of a Chemical Attack in Syria Is Overwhelming and Disturbing," *The Wire*, August 21, 2013, http://www.thewire.com/global/2013/08/visual-evidence-syrias-poison-gas-attack-overwhelming-and-disturbing/68586/.

threat against Syria, the country's credibility would be damaged, thereby emboldening U.S. enemies and shaking the faith of U.S. allies. Everyone in the administration, including the President, believed that the United States had to act.

According to a senior U.S. official, the Assad regime had been purposely increasing the number of deaths incurred by chemical weapons attacks as a way to test the U.S.'s commitment to its "red line" threat. Yet the administration avoided responding to the reported attacks in late 2012 and early 2013, providing no deterrent to keep Assad from escalating his use of chemical weapons. As John McCain puts it, "Assad was able to use chemical weapons before and there was no response, and so why not do it again? This should surprise no one...[Syria] viewed that not as a red line but as a green light..."[280] Members of the administration earlier revealed that the "red line" statement was made without an interagency process and that it was another message without a pre-existing or prepared strategy. Because of that, President Obama never "deliberately explained what his red line actually is and how it would change his calculus." A former defense policy advisor for President Obama was not convinced that the administration thought through the possible implications of such a statement. He said, "I am worried about the broader damage to U.S. credibility if we make a statement and then come back with lawyerly language to get around it."[281]

Those who knew how the Assad regime operated believed that the administration should have foreseen and prepared for the likelihood of an even deadlier chemical attack with the potential to draw the U.S. deeper into the Syrian conflict. Instead, in what one State Department official called an "inexplicable lack of policy preparation," the administration failed to draw up military contingency plans in the event that the U.S. was obligated to carry out its 2012 threat. Not only did the White House

---

[280]Josh Rogin, "Exclusive: McCain Says Obama Gave 'Green Light' to Syria to Use Chemical Weapons," *The Daily Beast*, August 27, 2013, http://www.thedailybeast.com/articles/2013/08/27/exclusive-mccain-says-obama-gave-green-light-to-syria-to-use-chemical-weapons.html.

[281]Baker et al.

lack trust in the Pentagon after a series of leaks, but it was also certain enough of its own aversion to military action that it did not bother to seek defense counsel.[282] In addition to all this, there was a significant degree of desensitization to the violence and chaos of the Syrian conflict among the members of the administration.[283] In a *New York Times* report, the overall atmosphere at the White House during meetings about Syria was described as very distracted and disinterested. The report stated, "Mr. Obama rarely voiced strong opinions during senior staff meetings. But current and former officials said his body language was telling: he often appeared impatient or disengaged while listening to the debate, sometimes scrolling through messages on his BlackBerry or slouching and chewing gum."[284] The same report also suggested that there were even some administration officials within Obama's inner circle that favored the status quo in Syria. Accordingly, "accompanying a group of senior lawmakers on a day trip to the Guantánamo Bay naval base in early June, Mr. McDonough argued that the status quo in Syria could keep Iran pinned down for years. In later discussions, he also suggested that a fight in Syria between Hezbollah and Al Qaeda would work to America's advantage, according to Congressional officials."[285] Although some of these officials changed their position as a result of deteriorating conditions in Syria, they nevertheless stayed skeptical about any form of engagement in Syria.

After the distribution of the videos of the chemical weapon attack, the first reaction from the White House came with a statement requesting immediate access to witnesses and affected individuals to examine and collect

[282]Glenn Thrush, "Locked in the Cabinet," *Politico Magazine,* November 2013, http://www.politico.com/magazine/story/2013/11/locked-in-the-cabinet-99374.html#ixzz38LJVdmds;

[283]Interview by Kilic Kanat, July 2014.

[284]Mark Mazzetti, Robert F. Worth and Michael R. Gordon, "Obama's Uncertain Path Amid Syria Bloodshed," *The New York Times,* October 22, 2013, http://mobile.nytimes.com/2013/10/23/world/middleeast/obamas-uncertain-path-amid-syria-bloodshed.html.

[285]Ibid; See also Peter Baker, "Amid Hunger Strike, Senators Lead Delegation to Prison at Guantánamo," *The Caucus* (New York Times blog), June 7, 2013, http://thecaucus.blogs.nytimes.com/2013/06/07/amid-hunger-strike-senators-lead-delegation-to-prison-at-guantanamo/.

physical evidence without any intervention from the Syrian government.[286] Meanwhile, the UNSC convened to discuss the attacks and potential responses to it. A major part of the international community focused on the U.S. reaction to the attacks, specifically due to Obama's "red line." The tone of the first White House statement also signaled an urgency and potential action by the United States. On the first day after the attack, the Obama administration stated that it could not verify the use of chemical weapons in Ghouta, requesting that intelligence agencies help confirm the allegations.[287] In an interview after the attacks, President Obama described the event as a "big event of grave concern." However, Obama also emphasized his cautiousness in deciding on a response to this episode. He explained, "Sometimes what we've seen is that folks will call for immediate action, jumping into stuff, that does not turn out well, gets us mired in very difficult situations, can result in us being drawn into very expensive, difficult, costly interventions that actually breed more resentment in the region."[288] The statement was clearly in the same pattern with the administration's previous positions on military interventions. He was expressing his caution and skepticism on the outcomes of the use of military force. For some Syrian observers, this statement itself was a major indicator of Washington's reluctance to take action.[289]

Over the next few days, President Obama and his administration reviewed the situation in Syria. Following these deliberations, Secretary of State John Kerry made a statement confirming that the White House held evidence on the use of chemical weapons in the suburbs of Damascus, including proof of the perpetrators. He stated,

[286]Martin Chulov, Mona Mahmood and Ian Sample, "Syria conflict: chemical weapons blamed as hundreds reported killed," *The Guardian*, August 22, 2013, http://www.theguardian.com/world/2013/aug/21/syria-conflcit-chemical-weapons-hundreds-killed.

[287]"U.S. says unable to conclusively determine chemical weapons used in Syria," *Reuters*, August 23, 2013, http://in.reuters.com/article/2013/08/22/syria-crisis-usa-state-idINDEE97L0IA20130822.

[288]"Obama: Syria chemical weapon claim a 'grave concern,'" *BBC News*, August 23, 2013, http://www.bbc.com/news/world-middle-east-23809409.

[289]Interview by Kilic Kanat, July 2014

"What has already happened in Syria is grounded in facts, informed by conscience and guided by common sense. The reported number of victims, the reported symptoms of those who were killed or injured, the firsthand accounts from humanitarian organizations on the ground, like Doctors Without Borders and the Syria Human Rights Commission—these all strongly indicate that everything these images are already screaming at us is real, that chemical weapons were used in Syria."[290]

The administration believed that the attack was conducted by the Assad regime, which possessed stockpiles of these weapons and had the ability to deliver such agents. Secretary Kerry also said that President Obama was working on making an informed decision on how to respond to these chemical attacks and that he believed that there must be accountability for those who perpetrated the attack.[291] At the same time, there was a debate occurring within the administration on how to respond to the attacks—whether to strike the regime immediately or whether to wait for UN inspectors to release their report.[292] While the administration was buying time with these discussions, several reports emerged suggesting that a conversation between an official at the Syrian Ministry of Defense and a leader of a chemical weapons unit had been intercepted. The content of the leak confirmed that the Assad regime was responsible for the chemical attack in Ghouta.[293] This was a major development since both the administration and international community were waiting for proof to verify that the Syrian regime was behind the attacks. In the meantime, the U.S. military began devising potential scenarios to "punish the Syrian regime," but the operations were limited ones. The goal was to take punitive action against the perpetrators of this crime, without tipping the balance in favor of the

---

[290]"Transcript: Secretary of State John Kerry's remarks on alleged Syria chemical attack," *The Washington Post,* August 26, 2013, http://www.washingtonpost.com/world/nation-security/transcript-secretary-of-state-john-kerrys-remarks-on-alleged-syria-chemical-attack/2013/08/26/40b-0b4ea-0e8b-11e3-bdf6-e4fc677d94a1_story.html.

[291]Ibid.

[292]Noah Shachtman, "Exclusive: Intercepted Calls Prove Syrian Army Used Nerve Gas, U.S. Spies Say," *Foreign Policy,* August 27, 2013, http://foreignpolicy.com/2013/08/27/exclusive-intercepted-calls-prove-syrian-army-used-nerve-gas-u-s-spies-say/.

[293]Ibid.

Syrian opposition or overthrowing the Assad regime. In fact, the White House wanted to continue to avoid involvement in the Syrian conflict and limit its goals to retaliation for the breach of international norms. According to the plan, the U.S. and its allies would use Tomahawk missiles to destroy Syrian command and control facilities, weapons delivery systems and intelligence bases to prevent the repetition of chemical attacks. The operation was planned to last for a narrow 48 hours, limited in nature with no boots on the ground or the imposition of a "no-fly zone."[294] However, even before its announcement, the plan generated a major debate among security analysts about its effectiveness. For instance, Chris Hammer, a former naval analyst who had earlier drafted a proposal for surgical strikes, expressed his skepticism about the success of such an operation under current circumstances. According to him, this form of tactical action was successful only in the presence of a clear strategic objective. In the absence of it, such actions could be pointless and counterproductive.[295] According to other security experts, the constant comments from the White House about the nature and length of the attacks were damaging their purpose. For David Deptula, the comments from the White House were just making it easier for Assad to prepare for the potential attacks, and thus, minimizing their possible impact.[296] Moreover, foreign policy experts were critical of the way that President Obama was handling the decision making process. David Rothkopf, in an article in *Foreign Policy*, interpreted the Obama administration's constant reaffirmation of the limited nature of the operations as a message that said, "We don't care so much if you kill your people. We primarily care *how* you kill your people."[297]

[294]Ibid.

[295]John Hudson, "Architect of Syria War Plan Doubts Surgical Strikes Will Work," *The Cable* (Foreign Policy blog), August 26, 2013, http://foreignpolicy.com/2013/08/26/architect-of-syria-war-plan-doubts-surgical-strikes-will-work/.

[296]Yochi Dreazen, "Did Obama Administration Leaks Already Spoil the Syria Attack?," *Foreign Policy*, August 28, 2013, http://foreignpolicy.com/2013/08/28/did-obama-administration-leaks-already-spoil-the-syria-attack/.

[297]David Rothkopf, "Too Little, Too Late," *Foreign Policy*, August 27, 2013, http://foreignpolicy.com/2013/08/27/too-little-too-late/.

With the release of the intelligence report, it was clear that the Obama administration held sufficient evidence that the Syrian regime was responsible for the chemical attacks.[298] Following the release of the report, Secretary Kerry delivered a speech to the American public, explaining the major findings and how the U.S. would respond accordingly. Once again, Kerry claimed that there would be no boots on the ground and that the operation would be limited to airstrikes. He was careful to distinguish the intervention in Syria from previous U.S. military involvement in the region. In addition, Kerry argued that the cost of inaction outweighed cost of action. He stated,

> "As previous storms in history have gathered, when unspeakable crimes were within our power to stop them, we have been warned against the temptations of looking the other way. History is full of leaders who have warned against inaction, indifference, and especially against silence when it mattered most. Our choices then in history had great consequences and our choice today has great consequences."[299]

The wording of Kerry's statement was pretty strong. He called Assad a "thug and a murderer" and expressed that the international community had the responsibility to act when there was such an obvious breach of international norms and humanitarian principles. According to him, the decision of the international community would have deep significance. He said, "It matters because if we choose to live in a world where a thug and a murderer like Bashar al-Assad can gas thousands of his own people with impunity, even after the United States and our allies said no, and then the world does nothing about it, there will be no end to the test of our resolve and the dangers that will flow from those others who believe that they can do as they will."[300]

---

[298]"Government Assessment of the Syrian Government's Use of Chemical Weapons on August 21, 2013," Press Release, August 30, 2012 (online by the White House Office of the Press Secretary), http://www.whitehouse.gov/the-press-office/2013/08/30/government-assessment-syrian-government-s-use-chemical-weapons-august-21.

[299]John Kerry, "Statement on Syria," Remarks, August 30, 2013 (online by U.S. Department of State), http://www.state.gov/secretary/remarks/2013/08/213668.htm.

[300]Ibid.

A day after Secretary Kerry's statement, President Obama made an announcement at the White House. Following several TV interviews with President Obama and the statements of Secretary Kerry, many around the world expected the President to explain the timing and nature of limited airstrikes. In his statement, President Obama claimed that he made the decision to take military action against regime targets. He also made it clear that it would not be an open-ended intervention and would not involve U.S. combat troops. He explained why it was important to degrade and destroy the regime's capacity to deliver chemical weapons for the U.S. and the international community. The President's statement was regarded as a declaration of the administration's intent to engage in a military operation until Obama surprised many with his footnote regarding the necessity to seek Congressional authorization to launch military strikes. He said, "Yet, while I believe I have the authority to carry out this military action without specific congressional authorization, I know that the country will be stronger if we take this course, and our actions will be even more effective."[301]

Later, David Rothkopf detailed how President Obama reached this decision. According to Rothkopf, it was again President Obama and his inner circle that made this critical decision without an interagency process or the involvement of key national security and foreign policy figures. Rothkopf stated that following the decision to launch a limited military strike,

> ...the president went on a walk around the South Lawn of the White House with his chief of staff, Denis McDonough, a longtime loyalist whose relationship with the president dates back to just prior to the 2008 campaign. McDonough was not just a chief of staff—he was a member of the president's tightly knit innermost circle and a former deputy national security advisor. McDonough had also long been one of the voices urging that America not get involved in Syria, often stiffening the commander in chief's resolve to keep out of the crisis when pressure came from others, such as first-term Secretary of State Hillary Clinton, who thought Washington ought to do more to support moderate opponents of Syrian President Bashar al-Assad. It was during their 45-minute stroll that Obama shared with McDonough his concerns about following through on his Syria plan.

[301]Obama, "Statement by the President on Syria," August 31, 2013.

Afterward, when the two joined a small group of top advisors in the Oval Office, Obama reportedly announced, "I have a big idea I want to run by you guys," and then segued into his new plan to put action on hold until he could get a formal vote of congressional support. Many in the group were stunned by the news, including Rice, who reportedly argued that it would send a message of vacillation and would set a bad precedent of deferring to Congress on such issues.

Notably, the group did not include several key national security principals. Obama called Hagel to let him know about the decision to punt. Absent as well was Kerry, whom Obama later privately informed about his change of mind. The secretary of state's team felt he had been treated badly, having been asked to play the role of front man on this issue just hours before.[302]

The announcement arrived at a moment of significant political polarization in the United States. It also sparked a debate within the U.S. about executive authority and presidential power. Previous presidents, including George H. Bush, Bill Clinton and Ronald Reagan, used limited force without seeking Congressional approval. Barack Obama himself conducted a military operation in Libya without seeking approval from Congress and he did not permit considerable Congressional involvement in his extensive drone strike campaign against terrorist targets in different countries around the world.[303] To seek an authorization before such a limited military strike could set a precedent and limit presidential powers in the future.[304] A few days after his statement, Obama went on to say during an interview, "As commander-in-chief I always preserve the right and the responsibility to act on behalf of America's national security…I do not believe that I was required to take this to Congress but I did not take this to Congress just because it's an empty exercise. I think it is important to have Congress's support."[305] As far as the international arena was con-

[302]David Rothkopf, "National Insecurity: Can Obama's Foreign Policy be Saved?" *Foreign Policy,* September 9, 2014, http://foreignpolicy.com/2014/09/09/national-insecurity/.

[303]William G. Howell, "All Syria Policy is Local," *Foreign Policy,* September 3, 2013, http://foreignpolicy.com/2013/09/03/all-syria-policy-is-local/.

[304]Karen DeYoung, "Obama's decision to turn to Congress on Syria decision triggers debate," *The Washington Post,* September 4, 2013, http://www.washingtonpost.com/world/national-security/obamas-decision-to-turn-to-congress-on-syria-decision-is-fodder-for-debate/2013/09/04/e59aace6-14ca-11e3-a100-66fa8fd9a50c_story.html.

[305]Dan Roberts, "Obama seeks global backing on Syria: 'I didn't set a red line. The world did,'" *The Guardian,* September 4, 2013, http://www.theguardian.com/world/2013/sep/04/obama-syria-red-line-chemical-weapons.

cerned, the decision to seek approval from Congress was not interpreted as a constitutional step, but rather as an attempt to delay and potentially avoid conducting military strikes.

In the meantime, a series of meetings were held between the administration and Congress in regards to the use of force in Syria. On the 3rd of September, President Obama met with Congressional leadership while Secretary Kerry, Secretary Hagel and General Dempsey testified at the Senate Foreign Relations Committee.[306] According to Hillary Clinton, during this process, she advised the president to secure symbolic support from Congress, while Russia and other countries—which were against a military intervention—watch warily to see what domestic political constraints would be placed on the Obama administration.[307] During the testimony of Secretary Kerry and Secretary Hagel, members of the administration tried to make the case for a military operation. For instance, Secretary Hagel stated, "A refusal to act would undermine the credibility of America's other security commitments—including the President's commitment to prevent Iran from acquiring a nuclear weapon. The word of the United States must mean something. It is vital currency in foreign relations and international and allied commitments."[308] More significantly, confusion began to appear in later days in regards to the nature of military operations and its targets. Although the administration was, until this declaration, very certain that it would be a limited military strikes, both the President and some leaders of Congress began to signal the presence of a broader strategy that would include overthrowing the Assad regime. First of all, President Obama, addressing the Congressional leadership, accentuated that his strategy for confronting the chemical weapons issue could strengthen the opposition, leading to a peaceful transition and generating stability for Syria and the

---

[306]"Full Transcript: Kerry, Hagel and Dempsey testify at Senate Foreign Relations Committee hearing on Syria," *The Washington Post*, September 3, 2013, http://www.washingtonpost.com/politics/running-transcript-senate-foreign-services-committee-hearing-on-syria/2013/09/03/35ae1048-14ca-11e3-b182-1b3bb2eb474c_story.html.

[307]Clinton, *Hard Choices*.

[308]Chuck Hagel, Statement on Syria before the Senate Foreign Relations Committee, Hearing, September 3, 2013, Available online at: http://www.defense.gov/Speeches/Speech.aspx?SpeechID=1802.

region. This was the first time that President Obama linked the planned military strikes to policy objectives.[309] Senator McCain, who had been a major proponent for more assertive action against the Assad regime, was also clear about his reservations on the current plan. McCain stated that President Obama, during his meeting with him, promised to include regime change as part of his strategy to on Syria's chemical weapons.[310]

It was a complicated scene for those who want to trace the process of decision making regarding Syria. Part of the convolution was due to the President's indecisiveness, which created a great deal of confusion among both the bureaucracy and observers of U.S. policy on Syria. Despite the week of painstaking deliberation, policy preparation and communication with allies that led to the decision to authorize the limited use of force, Obama chose to invite Congress to vote on the strike. Several reasons were provided for this sudden change of heart. For some, the failure to reach an agreement at the UNSC and the vote in the British parliament contributed to this re-evaluation.[311] However, almost all accounts of this period indicate that President Obama wanted Congress to take some responsibility in this critical decision so that if something went wrong, Congress could not criticize the President. Accordingly, following the disapproval of the administration's decision to use force in Libya from some members of Congress, the President decided to involve Congress in the decision making.[312] However, regardless of his motivation, the decision making process that President Obama conducted in this case demonstrates that he was making the decision himself and then consulting his aides on the operationalization of his unilateral plan.

---

[309]Dan Roberts and Spencer Ackerman, "Obama hints at larger strategy to topple Assad in effort to win over Republicans," *The Guardian,* September 3, 2013, http://www.theguardian.com/world/2013/sep/03/obama-strategy-assad-republicans-syria.

[310]Roberts, "Obama seeks global backing on Syria: 'I didn't set a red line. The world did.'"

[311]Dave Urbanski, "Obama Changed Mind at 11th Hour on Syria, Overriding Top National Security Advisers," *The Blaze,* August 31, 2013, http://www.theblaze.com/stories/2013/08/31/obama-changed-mind-at-11th-hour-on-syria-overriding-top-national-security-advisers-officials-say/.

[312]Howell, "All Syria Policy is Local."

In his public statements, the President claimed he altered the plan because a positive vote from Congress would strengthen the United States by offering Congress an olive branch and moving "forward together as one nation" on Syria.[313] Yet, some U.S. allies in the region as well as many members of the Syrian opposition saw the shift as an effort to backpedal on the plan, either to deflect blame in the event of failure or to use the polarized Congress to prevent its approval all together.[314] His backpedalling was also visible in his September 4th assertion that the U.S. "did not set a red line; the world set a red line."[315] With this statement, he was trying to argue that it was a global responsibility and thus it was not a burden for the United States to bear alone.

Obama, caught in a policy nightmare on the plausibility of airstrikes, was relieved when Russian President Vladimir Putin and Foreign Minister Sergei Lavrov offered him a peaceful egress from his dilemma in the name of global norms. The conversion seemed sudden: in a September 9th press conference, Kerry declared that if Assad wanted to prevent the bombing, "he could turn over every single bit of his chemical weapons to the international community in the next week...[but] it can't be done." Discussions in Washington over the reason of such a "proposal" spread among policy makers. For some within the State Department, it was a gaffe that Kerry made while trying to make the case that Assad could do nothing to prevent these punitive airstrikes. In fact, even the State Department was caught unprepared to handle such an announcement. Immediately after the statement, the State Department spokeswoman, in an email statement, stated,

> "Secretary Kerry was making a rhetorical argument about the impossibility and unlikelihood of Assad turning over chemical weapons he has denied he used...His (Kerry's) point was that this brutal dictator with a history of playing fast and loose with the facts cannot be trusted to turn over chemical weapons, otherwise he would have done so long ago. That's why the world faces this moment."[316]

[313] Urbanski, "Obama Changed Mind at the 11th Hour."

[314] Interview. Kilic Kanat August 2014

[315] Roberts, "Obama seeks global backing on Syria: 'I didn't set a red line. The world did.'"

[316] "State Department: Kerry Statement On Syria Turning Over Chemical Weapons Simply Rhetorical," *The Huffington Post*, September 9, 2013, http://www.huffingtonpost.com/2013/09/09/state-department-kerry-syria_n_3893213.html.

State Department officials were not informed about a change in plan. Following Kerry's statement, the predominant view was that the proposal would have no real impact on the Obama administration's plan.[317]

Yet, on September 10th, the Obama administration announced a deal with the Russians to do just that, a plan that had allegedly been in discussion for some time. He requested that Congress delay the vote on striking Syria and wait to see if another round of diplomacy on Syria with Russia would work. Russia proposed an agreement in which Syria would join the Chemical Weapons Convention and surrender its chemical arsenal to the Organization for the Prohibition of Chemical Weapons (OPCW) by mid-2014. The White House released a statement shortly after applauding the progress in negotiations on the elimination of chemical weapons.[318]

Following this agreement, Vice President Joe Biden labeled the agreement a credit to "President Barack Obama's "absolutely clear" vision for foreign policy."[319] Thus, the prospect of military intervention in Syria essentially put to rest, as the United States joined forces with Russia in a UN draft resolution calling on Assad to relinquish his chemical weapons. Syria agreed to the deal, which the Obama administration identified as a direct result of the "credible threat of U.S. force."[320] The deal received criticism, as many believed it lent Assad legitimacy and emboldened his actions. The debate in regards to Syria was diverted and monopolized by the issue of chemical weapons. As October came to an end, Secretary Kerry released a statement emphasizing the success of the first phase of the destruction of Syria's chemical weapons.[321]

---

[317]Interview by Kilic Kanat, July 2014.

[318]Barack Obama, "Statement by the President on U.S.-Russian Agreement on Framework for Elimination of Syrian Chemical Weapons," Press Release, September 14, 2013, (online by the White House Office of the Press Secretary), http://www.whitehouse.gov/the-press-office/2013/09/14/statement-president-us-russian-agreement-framework-elimination-syrian-ch.

[319]Alexander Burns, "Joe Biden credits Obama on Syria," *Politico*, September 15, 2013, http://www.politico.com/story/2013/09/joe-biden-syria-96825.html.

[320]Dan Roberts and Julian Borger, "Vladimir Putin warns US not to launch attack in Syria," *The Guardian*, September 12, 2013, http://www.theguardian.com/world/2013/sep/12/putin-warns-us-not-to-attack-syria.

[321]John Kerry, "Progress Eliminating Syria's Chemical Weapons Program," Press Release, October 31, 2013 (online by the U.S. Department of State), http://www.state.gov/secretary/remarks/2013/10/216143.htm.

While the chemical weapons were being destroyed, the Assad regime continued its attacks on civilians by using conventional weapons. The agreement was likely perceived by the Assad regime as a green light to continue its operations using conventional weapons. In the meantime, after the President's last minute change of heart, Secretary Kerry turned back to diplomacy. In October, he resumed the preparation for an international conference that would bring together the regime and Assad forces for the first time. However, in the fall of 2013, Secretary Kerry's initiative had to be postponed because of the difficulty in bringing together separate groups, and more significantly, as many in the State Department believed that it could lead to a humiliating situation for the United States.[322] Furthermore, many actors in the region believed that it would be a futile endeavor and would not bring a solution to the conflict in Syria.

In the meantime, because of the fluid situation on the ground in Syria, there were several signs of change in U.S. policy in regards to the opposition forces. First, in November, seven different Islamic groups came together and formed the Islamic Front, which became a significant center of power on the ground. Although the U.S. did not consider the Islamic Front a terrorist organization, like al-Nusra, the administration was concerned about the anti-American and anti-Western opinions and the Salafi backgrounds of some members. In a short period of time, the Islamic Front gained control of several FSA bases. Following this development, State Department Spokeswoman Marie Harf responded to a question by stating that the U.S. was open to engagement with the Islamic Front. She mentioned that the U.S. "wouldn't rule out the possibility of meeting with the Islamic Front," and "can engage with the Islamic Front, of course, because they're not designated terrorists." Harf also said that the U.S. was open to meet different opposition groups.[323] In the meantime, *Reuters* reported that U.S.

[322]Yochi Dreazen, "Exclusive: Kerry and Top State Dept Officials Split Over Syria Talks," *The Cable* (Foreign Policy blog), October 23, 2013, http://foreignpolicy.com/2013/10/23/exclusive-kerry-and-top-state-dept-officials-split-over-syria-talks/.

[323]John Hudson, "U.S. Weighing Closer Ties With Hard-Line Islamists in Syria," *The Cable* (Foreign Policy blog), December 17, 2013, http://foreignpolicy.com/2013/12/17/u-s-weighing-closer-ties-with-hardline-islamists-in-syria/.

officials and Islamic Front leaders were scheduled to meet in Turkey at the same time as Ambassador Ford was expected to visit Turkey.[324] According to some within the Syrian opposition, the main goal of the meeting was to bring together the Islamic Front and the FSA under a single command in order to create a unified command structure.[325] Although early contacts with the group proved inconclusive, it was nevertheless considered a major step in U.S. policy on Syria.[326]

With the beginning of 2014, U.S. diplomats sped up the preparation for the Geneva II Conference, which was expected by certain members of the U.S. government to be the first step in launching a process of negotiation between the opposition and the Assad regime. During this time, the growing crisis in Ukraine had become the biggest distraction for the State Department officials' efforts to organize the conference. The international conference took place in Switzerland in the last week of January. Securing the attendance of the Syrian opposition was a serious accomplishment on the part of Secretary Kerry.[327] Kerry, in his introductory remarks, underlined the significance of the negotiations to reach an agreement on a transition government. He stated,

> "Mutual consent, which is what has brought us here, for a transition government means that that government cannot be formed with someone that is objected to by one side or the other. That means that Bashar Assad will not be part of that transition government. There is no way – no way possible in the imagination – that the man who has led the brutal response to his own people could regain the legitimacy to govern. One man and those who have supported him can no longer hold an entire nation and a region hostage. The right to lead a country does not come from torture, nor barrel bombs, nor Scud missiles.

[324]Mariam Karouny and Dasha Afanasieva, "Syrian Islamist rebels to meet U.S. officials: opposition sources," *Reuters,* December 14, 2013, http://www.reuters.com/article/2013/12/14/us-syria-crisis-rebels-idUSBRE9BD08D20131214.

[325]Hudson, "U.S. Weighing Closer Ties With Hard-Line Islamists in Syria."

[326]Scott Lucas, "Syria: US Shifts Position — Again — on Co-operation with Islamic Front," *EA WorldView,* December 13, 2013, http://eaworldview.com/2013/12/syria-us-shifts-position-co-operation-islamic-front/.

[327]Joyce Karam, "Syria's Geneva II is a win for Kerry with 'zero chance' for transition," *Al-Arabiya,* January 23, 2014, http://english.alarabiya.net/en/perspective/analysis/2014/01/23/Syria-s-Geneva-II-is-a-win-for-Kerry-with-zero-chance-for-transition.html.

It comes from the consent of the people. And it's hard to imagine how that consent could be forthcoming at this point in time.

So just as there could be no place for the perpetrator of this violence, there could also be no place for the thousands of violent extremists who spread their hateful ideology and worsen the suffering of the Syrian people. And as we hear talk about terrorism today, make no mistake: It is the presence of the current intransigence within the existing government that makes this problem worse. That is creating a magnet for terrorists. And until a transition takes place, there is no prayer of reducing the increase of terrorism."[328]

Despite the recognition of his efforts to bring together this conference, most people did not expect the conference to result in any agreement or the formation of a transition government. As expected, after a week, the conference ended with no significant outcome.

With the failure of the Geneva II process, the administration shelved the discourse about finding a diplomatic solution to the crisis in Syria for a certain period of time. Administration officials still underlined that there could be no military solution for the conflict in Syria; however, those who recently left the administration, such as Fred Hof, who had served as special advisor for the transition in Syria, demonstrated that there were some serious disagreements within the Obama administration on this issue. After leaving his post, Hof criticized the administration for constantly emphasizing that there could be no military solution. Immediately after the end of Geneva II meetings, he stated,

"Those who say there is no military solution for Syria are really saying there are no military options they wish to exercise. Even the modest, life-saving option of destroying regime air, artillery, rocket, and missile assets used to produce genocidal effects is dismissed on the grounds that it cannot solve the overall problem of Syria. As President Obama recently claimed in The New Yorker, the choice is all or nothing: invade and occupy Iraq-style or refrain entirely from military strikes. Why is this so? What was he considering last August before he changed his mind? Did the anti-genocide bombing campaign in Serbia a decade-and-a-half ago aim to occupy the country?"[329]

[328]"Transcript: John Kerry's remarks at Geneva II conference on Syria on Jan. 22,' *The Washington Post,* January 22, 2014, http://www.washingtonpost.com/world/transcript-john-kerrys-remarks-at-geneva-ii-conference-on-syria-on-jan-22/2014/01/22/f2ec3a56-83b8-11e3-bbe5-6a2a3141e3a9_story.html.

[329]Frederic C. Hof, "Syria: What Next for Geneva II?" *MENASource* (Atlantic Council blog), February 3, 2014, http://www.atlanticcouncil.org/blogs/menasource/syria-what-next-for-geneva-ii.

According to media reports, Secretary Kerry started to express his frustration more vocally in various meetings. Leaks from a closed-door meeting at the security conference in Munich between Secretary Kerry and senior senators strengthened this perception. According to reports, Secretary Kerry was frustrated with the lack of success of the current policy on Syria and expressed concerns regarding the increasing number of extremists streaming into the region. Those present at the meeting, including Senator Graham and Senator McCain, stated that Secretary Kerry emphasized the need for a new strategy and the necessity of boosting the capacity of the opposition.[330] Although it was immediately denied by the State Department, most pundits in Washington, DC believed that there was indeed a need for a new strategy. They agreed that the President Obama's approach of reaching out to Russia and finding a diplomatic solution had proven to be ineffective in degrading or stopping Assad's forces.

Starting from February onwards, the use of military strikes to weaken the Syrian regime and training opposition forces was back on the table. In this instance, the main sponsor of the plan was Secretary Kerry. Partly because of the failure of the Geneva II process and partly as a result of the delays in the elimination of chemical weapons, Secretary Kerry consulted with Generals David Petraeus and Jack Keane. These generals stated that a limited military strikes together with the training and equipping of the opposition forces would be a good way to go. According to a *Wall Street Journal* report, Kerry proposed this idea to the White House and his main ally in this endeavor was U.S. Ambassador to the U.N. Samantha Power, well known for her role in Libya and her advocacy of humanitarian interventionism. Referring to a senior administration official, *The Wall Street Journal* reported, "Kerry has felt that diplomacy backed by the threat of force is an effective approach and that it would strengthen the administration's hand, but he has never felt that we have run out of diplomatic op-

---

[330]Michael R. Gordon and Mark Mazzetti, "U.S. Spy Chief Says Assad Has Strengthened His Hold on Power," *The New York Times,* February 4, 2014, http://www.nytimes.com/2014/02/05/world/middleeast/us-representative-to-syrian-opposition-is-retiring.html?_r=0.

tions—this will only be resolved through diplomacy."[331] However, during the meeting on Kerry's plan, Secretary Hagel and Chairman of the Joint Chiefs of Staff Martin Dempsey opposed the plan and convinced Kerry to postpone it. For Dempsey, even a very limited military intervention in the Syrian conflict could possibly suck the U.S. into a prolonged struggle whereas, for Hagel, the real problem was how to vet the opposition forces to train. Furthermore, Pentagon officials were also concerned about the train and equip program for the Syrian opposition, since such an endeavor could jeopardize the process of eliminating Syria's chemical weapons.[332] This situation demonstrated, unlike the case of Clinton's plan to arm opposition groups, that there was a serious difference of opinion between the Pentagon and the State Department over the best policy for Syria.

Although President Obama's position in this debate has not been made public, there were important indications on his stance. Especially in his interviews with David Remnick, President Obama expressed his opposition to both military intervention and arming and equipping the moderate rebels. President Obama considered U.S. action in Syria as a gateway for a disaster similar to that of Iraq. In the interview, he said, "I am not haunted by my decision not to engage in another Middle Eastern war. It is very difficult to imagine a scenario in which our involvement in Syria would have led to a better outcome, short of us being willing to undertake an effort in size and scope similar to what we did in Iraq."[333] President Obama also responded to criticism over not helping the Syrian opposition by stating, "When I hear people suggesting that somehow if we had just financed and armed the opposition earlier, that somehow Assad would be gone by now and we'd have a peaceful transition, it's magical thinking."[334] With these

[331]Adam Entous and Julian E. Barnes, "John Kerry, U.S. Military Clash on Approach to Syria's Rebels," *The Wall Street Journal,* April 7, 2014, http://www.wsj.com/articles/SB10001424052 702304441304579479500649988892.

[332]Ibid.

[333]David Remnick, "Going the Distance," *The New Yorker,* January 27, 2014, http://www. newyorker.com/magazine/2014/01/27/going-the-distance-2?currentPage=all.

[334]Ibid.

statements, President Obama actually closed the door to different forms of interventions offered by different administration officials. Fred Hof, in an essay discussing the interview, wrote that President Obama was not willing to even evaluate any other options and equated every form of military intervention with the Iraqi experience. Because of this, the only alternative for him seemed inaction.[335] In the same essay, Hof also described Obama's arguments against arming the opposition by writing, "This is a straw man fallacy that misrepresents the views of those who have opposed the arm's-length, rhetoric-rich hope that Syria could somehow fix itself if only the warring parties would meet and sort things out. The real question is what the balance on the ground would look like now in Syria if the president had heeded the advice of his national security team in the summer of 2012."[336] The arguments that President Obama made during the interview made it pretty clear that he had not changed his position on Syria.

During the first months of 2014, Syria was placed on the agenda because of increasing reports of radicalism in the region. As stated above, Secretary Kerry emphasized during the Geneva Conference that the region was becoming "a magnet for terrorists" because of the policies of the Syrian government. This statement was later repeated by the Director of National Intelligence, James Clapper, in a Senate Intelligence Committee hearing. Clapper stated that Syria had become a huge magnet for terrorists for both recruitment and training.[337] A few weeks after Obama's interview, the director of CIA, John Brennan, issued a statement that conflict with those of the President. During a hearing, Brennan went on to state that the situation in Syria had created a fertile ground for organizations such as al-Qaeda to emerge and organize attacks in and alongside the Syrian bor-

[335]Frederic C. Hof, "Syria: The Shadow of Iraq," *MENASource* (Atlantic Council blog), January 27, 2014, http://www.atlanticcouncil.org/blogs/menasource/syria-the-shadow-of-iraq.

[336]Ibid.

[337]John Hudson, "Intel Chiefs: Syria a 'Huge Magnet' for International Terrorists," *The Cable* (Foreign Policy blog), January 29, 2014, http://foreignpolicy.com/2014/01/29/intel-chiefs-syria-a-huge-magnet-for-international-terrorists/.

der.[338] Following this, Homeland Security Secretary Jeh Johnson stressed that the civil war in Syria had become a threat for the U.S. homeland security.[339] However, especially in regards to rising threats such as ISIS, President Obama was less inclined to consider them a major potential threat. Responding to a question in regards to ISIS, the President said,

> "The analogy we use around here sometimes, and I think is accurate, is if a jayvee team puts on Lakers uniforms that doesn't make them Kobe Bryant....I think there is a distinction between the capacity and reach of a bin Laden and a network that is actively planning major terrorist plots against the homeland versus jihadists who are engaged in various local power struggles and disputes, often sectarian." [340]

Following this he also emphasized,

> "Let's just keep in mind, Falluja is a profoundly conservative Sunni city in a country that, independent of anything we do, is deeply divided along sectarian lines. And how we think about terrorism has to be defined and specific enough that it doesn't lead us to think that any horrible actions that take place around the world that are motivated in part by an extremist Islamic ideology are a direct threat to us or something that we have to wade into."[341]

Both of these statements later generated a great deal of criticism of Obama and the administration's approach to the early signals of ISIS' presence in Iraq and Syria. The statements also demonstrated that there was mismatch between the intelligence community and the White House.

Just before the summer, media reports provided details about the delivery of U.S. antitank missiles to an opposition group. According to these reports, two dozens U.S.-made TOW missiles were provided to moderate opposition groups by the Friends of Syria. This was part of the pilot program, observed as the introduction of a potentially larger flow of sophisticated weaponry in the very near future. The TOWs that were giv-

---

[338]Michael R. Gordon and Mark Mazzetti, "U.S. Spy Chief Says Assad Has Strengthened His Hold on Power," *The New York Times,* February 4, 2014, http://www.nytimes.com/2014/02/05/world/middleeast/us-representative-to-syrian-opposition-is-retiring.html?_r=0.

[339]"Homeland security secretary: Syria conflict a threat to U.S.," *CBS News,* February 7, 2014, http://www.cbsnews.com/news/homeland-security-secretary-syria-conflict-a-threat-to-united-states/.

[340]Remnick, "Going the Distance."

[341]Ibid.

en to opposition groups in early March had extra security mechanisms, including fingerprint-keyed security devices. The only statement from the White House said, "The U.S. is committed to building the capacity of the moderate opposition, including through the provision of assistance to the vetted members of the moderate armed opposition."[342] The observers of U.S. policy on Syria, including Andrew Tabler and Fred Hof, interpreted this recent development as a signal of a major change in U.S. policy in the region, particularly its relations with armed opposition groups.[343] However, in the coming weeks and months, there were no other reports about the continuation of this effort. It was largely a one-time deal. Later, some members of the Syrian opposition stated that those who delivered the missiles asked the opposition members to record and post their use of these missiles on social media. It was not very clear why this was demanded from the armed opposition but it was interpreted as more of a PR move than a change in strategic thinking.[344] A few weeks later, a statement by General Martin Dempsey also demonstrated that there was no major change in the approach to the Syrian opposition. In a panel at the Atlantic Council, Dempsey responded to a question about the Syrian opposition's demands for anti-aircraft weaponry. He stated that such assistance would be a short-term solution for the problem on the ground and described the future of Syria as a series of crises and conflicts.[345]

In the summer of 2014, the Obama administration tried to pass a resolution at the UNSC to authorize an ICC investigation into the Syrian regime because of its crimes and the evidence about mass atrocities com-

[342]Ellen Knickmeyer, Maria Abi-Habib And Adam Entous, "Advanced U.S. Weapons Flow to Syrian Rebels," *The Wall Street Journal*, April 18, 2014, http://www.wsj.com/articles/SB10001 424052702304626304579509401865454762.

[343]Matthew Bell, "Why are US-made anti-tank missiles showing up in Syria?," *PRI*, April 17, 2014, http://www.pri.org/stories/2014-04-17/why-are-us-made-anti-tank-missiles-showing-syria.

[344]Interview by Kilic Kanat, July 2014.

[345]John Hudson, "Top U.S. General: Syrian Opposition Not Ready for the Big Leagues," *The Cable* (Foreign Policy blog), May 14, 2014, http://foreignpolicy.com/2014/05/14/top-u-s-gener-al-syrian-opposition-not-ready-for-the-big-leagues/.

mitted by Assad's forces. However, the resolution was vetoed by Russia and China. After the vote, Samantha Power made a statement expressing her disappointment with the outcome and the commitment of the U.S. to help those being persecuted.[346] There was also increasing signs of frustration within the administration. During a May visit by the Syrian opposition to Washington—of which the content was leaked to the press a few days later—Secretary Kerry reiterated his frustration about the Syrian impasse, revealing yet another major disagreement within the administration. Reportedly, in a private meeting with the leaders of the Syrian opposition, Secretary Kerry disclosed that he believed the international community wasted a year by failing to coordinate in concert to topple Bashar al-Assad.[347] What is particularly important was that while the administration was signaling a potential reevaluation of its Syria policy, senior members of the administration seemed to be extremely frustrated with the lack of any development. Some members of the opposition who were present in the meeting stated that Kerry was more vocal in his frustration; however, they also said that Kerry was ultimately not the decision-maker and that the power to act did not lay in his hands.[348]

In May, President Obama delivered a speech at West Point, in which he mostly focused on foreign policy and security challenges that the U.S. was facing in the world. Obama, after restating his belief that there was no military solution to the conflict, signaled again a potential policy change by saying that he was planning to help those who could be an alternative to both terrorists and a brutal dictator at the same time. He said,

> "As frustrating as it is, there are no easy answers – no military solution that can eliminate the terrible suffering anytime soon. As President, I made

[346]Samantha Powers, "Explanation of Vote by Ambassador Samantha Power, U.S. Permanent Representative to the United Nations, On the Security Council Vote on Syria," Press Release, May 22, 2014 (online by the United States Mission to the United Nations), http://usun.state.gov/briefing/statements/226438.htm.

[347]Josh Rogin, "Exclusive: Kerry Told Syrian Rebels 'We Wasted a Year' in Fight Against Assad," *The Daily Beast*, May 12, 2014, http://www.thedailybeast.com/articles/2014/05/12/exclusive-kerry-told-syrian-rebels-we-wasted-a-year-in-fight-against-assad.html.

[348]Interview by Kilic Kanat, January 2015

a decision that we should not put American troops into the middle of this increasingly sectarian civil war, and I believe that is the right decision. But that does not mean we shouldn't help the Syrian people stand up against a dictator who bombs and starves his people. And in helping those who fight for the right of all Syrians to choose their own future, we also push back against the growing number of extremists who find safe-haven in the chaos.

With the additional resources I'm announcing today, we will step up our efforts to support Syria's neighbors – Jordan and Lebanon; Turkey and Iraq – as they host refugees, and confront terrorists working across Syrian borders. I will work with Congress to ramp up support for those in the Syrian opposition who offer the best alternative to terrorists and a brutal dictator."[349]

Again, although it was not completely clear how this policy change would be operationalized in the coming months, this statement was considered a potentially serious signal of a shift in U.S. policy. Some observers stated that there might be a serious reconsideration of the future of U.S. policy on Syria after these remarks.[350] While these considerations were underway, Mosul, the second largest city in Iraq, was taken over by ISIS, shocking the administration and the international community. Although some considered this development a source of distraction for the Obama administration, observers like Hof—writing about developments in Syria—argued that it could be a great opportunity for revising the Syria policy and working with the FSA to change the course of the conflict in the country and resist the rise of ISIS and the Assad regime at the same time.[351] While President Obama signaled this change of course, at the same time, he continued to express his skepticism about the capability of the moderate opposition groups in Syria. Answering a question on this issue, President Obama stated,

"Oftentimes, the challenge is if you have former farmers or teachers or pharmacists who now are taking up opposition against a battle-hardened re-

[349]Abby Ohlheiser, "President Obama Says His Foreign Policy Critics Are 'Misreading History,'" *The Wire*, May 28, 2014, http://www.thewire.com/politics/2014/05/watch-live-president-obama-addresses-his-foreign-policy-critics/371700/.

[350]Michael Gerson, "Michael Gerson: The end of illusions," *The Washington Post*, June 12, 2014, http://www.washingtonpost.com/opinions/michael-gerson-the-end-of-illusions/2014/06/12/0ff2bf24-f25b-11e3-914c-1fbd0614e2d4_story.html.

[351]Frederic C. Hof, "Syria: The Impact of ISIS in Iraq," *MENASource* (Foreign Policy blog), June 13, 2014, http://www.atlanticcouncil.org/blogs/menasource/syria-the-impact-of-isis-in-iraq.

gime, with support from external actors that have a lot at stake, how quickly can you get them trained; how effective are you able to mobilize them. And that continues to be a challenge."[352]

This was the second time that the President portrayed the moderate Syrian opposition in these terms. He mostly used this argument to explain his reluctance to engage in train and equip operations. For him, it was unrealistic to expect these people to make a difference on the ground even if they were being supported and equipped by the United States. This constant emphasis on the opposition's incapability was harshly criticized by former members of the administration. For instance, in an essay criticized this position, Hof stated,

> The question that arises, however, is why President Obama fails to mention the tens of thousands of Syrian Army officers and soldiers who abandoned the Assad regime rather than participate in that regime's campaign of mass homicide. Why is the totality of what the president calls "the moderate opposition" characterized by him as entirely civilian, and therefore inadequate, in nature? And why does he *not* assume that a healthy percentage of the farmers, teachers, pharmacists, dentists, and radio reporters to whom he refers have had significant prior military training as conscripts in Syria? Does he think that Syria has had an all-volunteer military force for the past fifty years?
>
> The president and his strategic communications people should drop this alibi. It is inaccurate, unworthy, and patronizing, if not insulting. Yes, Syrians from all walks of life have rebelled against a regime that exploits their labor, assaults their dignity, and assigns to their lives and well-being a sub-human status. Among those who have taken up arms there are, no doubt, some who have had to learn for the first time about the business end of an AK-47. And even those in uniform who walked away from the Assad killing machine were not the recipients of world-class military training. Yet to imply that Syrians who have taken up arms to defend themselves are coming directly from the stable or the library to the battlefield is inaccurate. It is also gratuitously damaging to President Obama in the eyes of Syrians. One wonders, however, if he cares.[353]

There were other voices that raised similar concerns about Obama's handling of the Syria crisis and the potential impact on the situation on

[352]Barack Obama, "Remarks by the President on the Situation in Iraq," Press Release, June 19, 2014 (online by the White House Office of the Press Secretary), http://www.whitehouse.gov/the-press-office/2014/06/19/remarks-president-situation-iraq.

[353]Frederic C. Hof, "Syria: Farmers, Teachers, Pharmacists, and Dentists," *MENASource* (Foreign Policy blog), June 20, 2014, http://www.atlanticcouncil.org/blogs/menasource/syria-farmers-teachers-pharmacists-and-dentists.

the ground if President Obama would arm and equip the moderate rebels. While trying to respond to these claims, President Obama constantly re-emphasized that the moderate opposition was nothing but a "bunch of ordinary civilians" who had no experience or training in fighting against Syria's battle-hardened military. In an interview in late June, President Obama stated, "When you get farmers, dentists, and folks who have never fought before going up against a ruthless opposition in Assad, the notion that they were in a position to suddenly overturn not only Assad but also ruthless, highly trained jihadists if we just sent a few arms is a fantasy."[354]

On June 26, 2014, a significant development took place in U.S. policy. The President asked Congress for an unexpected $500 million to train and arm the moderate opposition in Syria. The plan was an important turning point in terms of signaling yet another change in the policy of the administration. According to media reports, the program would be affiliated with the Defense Department instead of CIA.[355] However, observers of the Syria policy were extremely cautious in evaluating such a move without seeing its full implementation by the Pentagon. According to one Democratic senator, the White House had only sent emails, not envoys, to Congress in order to court their favor for the proposal.[356] Moreover, there had been little movement from the administration to fund any programs to address the problem. Until August 2014, U.S. policy had not been enough to change the tide of the conflict, but whatever moderate effort the United States made could be considered a small step in the right direction.

[354]"Obama: Notion that Syrian opposition could have overthrown Assad with U.S. arms a 'fantasy,'" *CBS News,* June 20, 2014, http://www.cbsnews.com/news/obama-notion-that-syrian-opposition-could-overthrow-assad-a-fantasy/.

[355]Julian E. Barnes, Adam Entous and Carol Lee, "U.S. Set To Train, Arm Syria Rebels," *The Wall Street Journal,* June 27, 2014, http://online.wsj.com/news/articles/SB20001424052702304557404579648751596692202.

[356]Interview by Kilic Kanat, July 2014.

CONCLUSION: ISIS AND THE NEW ERA IN U.S. POLICY ON SYRIA

During the summer of 2014, there was no announced plan on how to handle ISIS and simultaneously control the conflict in Syria, despite the fact that the Syrian conflict was the main source of the rise of the ISIS and other extremist groups in the region. Two particular developments in the region completely shifted international attention from the conflict in Syria to ISIS. First, ISIS' siege of Erbil mobilized U.S. policy makers to take serious steps towards action against the ISIS. With this significant development, the administration started to approach ISIS as more of an Iraqi problem, rather than bringing together a comprehensive strategy that would resolve the conflict in Syria, which was regarded as a magnet for radical groups by the highest levels of the Obama administration for the past year. A second development took place again in the month of August. After airstrikes had begun to be carried out by the international coalition, ISIS executed an American journalist, James Foley. The beheading was recorded by ISIS and distributed through social media. It was the first time since 9/11 that the U.S. public had witnessed the visual presentation of a terrorist attack, creating a major debate among policy makers in Washington, DC. In a very short period of time, this development transformed the discussion about ISIS and the region into a debate on terrorism. A few weeks after this incident, ISIS executed another American hostage, Steven Sotloff, by beheading him and circulating the record on social media. These two videos shocked both the American public and policy makers in the United States. Terrorism then became the predominant agenda in regards to the region. Following these attacks, President Obama once again stirred controversy about his policy on Syria by stating that the U.S. still had no strategy to deal with ISIS in Syria.[357] Although President Obama

---

[357]Tom Cohen, "Obama's no 'strategy yet' comment on ISIS in Syria sparks a political uproar," *CNN*, August 29, 2014, http://edition.cnn.com/2014/08/29/politics/obama-isis-strategy/.

announced a strategy to fight ISIS a few weeks after this statement, the new strategy also lacked elements to deal with the Assad regime.

Different factors and variables have shaped U.S. policy on Syria since the beginning of the crisis four years ago. However, several previous decisions in U.S. foreign policy and prior military interventions always played a very significant role in the administration's decision making. First of all, as Aaron David Miller stated in different articles, the priority for President Obama was the American middle class, not the Middle East. Thus, he did not want to engage in a conflict in the region, regardless of the scale of the tragedy occurring on the ground. The war in Iraq and its aftermath always haunted the President and his inner circle, who began to consider a potential intervention in Syria as a pathway to another Iraq. Secondly, Russia's engagement in the conflict, its vetoes at the UNSC and its support for the Syrian regime depleted the administration's appetite to engage in the Syrian civil war. On the one hand, any intervention would contradict President Obama's first term policy of resetting U.S. foreign affairs. On the other hand, another proxy war with Russia was not something the U.S. was willing to launch. This also reminded some in Washington, DC of the war in Afghanistan. Of course the situation in Ukraine further complicated the situation. Thirdly, the nuclear negotiations with Iran were considered a significant foreign policy and national security priority for the Obama administration. According to some experts, any intervention in Syria was avoided because of the reluctance of the White House to complicate matters with the Iranian government. Finally, the events in Libya, especially the killing of the U.S. ambassador after an attack on the embassy in Benghazi, generated great uncertainty for the Obama administration. Of course, there are other arguments to explain the Obama administration's inaction in Syria. After a few years, with more memoirs, analysis and leaks, we will undoubtedly learn more about the rationale of President Obama in regards to Syria. However, the explanations offered above are the most significant for understanding President Obama's actions towards the conflict in Syria for the first four years.

A final question remains about the decision making structure of the Obama administration in regards to the conflict in Syria. After the publication of the memoirs of former administration officials, including Hillary Clinton, Leon Panetta, Vali Nasr and Robert Gates, as well as several other investigative studies on Syria by journalists and analysts, such as David Rothkopf and David Sanger, it is clear that the majority of the decision making power on Syria policy lies with the President himself and his inner circle. Yet, in his efforts to deliberate, analyze and rehash the policy in Syria, it seems that the President has become more of a "Professor-in-Chief," as David Remnick has called him, than the military and political leader of the United States.[358] Thus far, U.S. policy on Syria has been handled by a small group of advisors, including those who have been with President Obama since the beginning of his political career, such as Deputy National Security Advisor Ben Rhodes and Chief of Staff Denis McDonough. Nevertheless, according to the pattern, nothing can easily change President Obama's calculus on Syria.

Since President Obama's inauguration in 2009, U.S. foreign policy in Syria has been shaped by his deliberative and centralized structure of decision making. Although the administration demonstrated overall unity in its Syria policy at the outset of Obama's first term, events since the outbreak of the conflict in 2011 have forged a cleavage between the interagency bureaucracy and the White House over the appropriate degree of U.S. involvement. Ultimately, President Obama and his closest advisors—haunted by the specter of Iraq and overwhelmed by domestic political pressures—pursued their own policy imperatives in determining the United States' stance on the conflict. As a result, U.S. policy has lacked cohesion, strategy and impact. Because of that, pundits in Washington, DC and former members of the Obama administration believe that nothing will change in U.S. policy towards Syria until a new administration moves in the White House in 2016...

[358]Pfiffner, "Decision Making in the Obama White House."; See also Remnick, "Going the Distance."

TIMELINE OF U.S.-SYRIA RELATIONS
(JANUARY 2009 TO JUNE 2014)

October 26, 2008   U.S. troops allegedly descend from helicopters to attack Al-Sukkariya, a Syrian enclave five miles west of the Iraqi city Qaim to kill Badran Turki Hishan al -Mazidih - Iraqi sanctioned by U.S. Treasury for allowing supplies to funnel to AQI through Syria. Demonstrated that U.S. taking matters into own hands to address AQI in Syria.[359]

November 2008   Pres. Obama is elected amidst the suspension of indirect Syrian-Israeli negotiations in reaction to Israel's 2008-2009 Operation Cast Lead in Gaza. Bashar al-Assad declares that Israel's attack on Gaza in December 2008 "closed the door on the Syrian-Israeli indirect talks." Later, the Syria pushes other arab countries to stop endorsing the Arab Peace Initiative with Israel, sponsored by Saudi Arabia. Assad joins Hezbollah and Iran in backing Hamas' call for Israel to unconditionally open its border crossings with Gaza.[360]

November 2008   Sami Moubayed authors an article about the steps Obama would have to take to court Syrian favor. This included:

1) Reinstitution of a U.S. ambassador in Damascus
2) An end to the anti-Syrian rhetoric from the White House and State Department, which had been harsh since 2003
3) Recognition of Syria's attempt to help border security
4) Assistance in some form to help with 1.2 million Iraqi refugees
5) Lifting of sanctions on Damascus
6) Abolition of Syrian Accountability Act
7) Willingness to hold indirect peace talks with Israel
8) Recognition that no problems in Mid-East can be solved without Syria
9) Combat against Islamic fundamentalism
10) Apology for air raid on Syria that left 8 dead in October 2008 and
11) Normalization of relations between Syria and America on a people-to-people level.

---

[359]Tabler, *In the Lion's Den*, 215.

[360]Sharp, "Syria: Background and U.S. Relations," 2-3.

November 19, 2008   IAEA puts Syria on its agenda for the al-Kibar reactor.[361]

February 9, 2009   U.S. Department of Commerce eases restrictions on an export license for Boeing 747 spare parts to Syrian Air, Syria's national airline.[362]

February 26, 2009   Jeff Feltman, Assistant Sec. of State, and Daniel Shapiro, Middle East expert of the NSC meet with the Syrian Ambassador to the U.S. (Imad Mustapha) to address U.S. concerns about Syrian behavior. Pres. Obama asks Clinton to arrange this meeting 1) to engage with America's adversaries as the underpinning idea of U.S. foreign policy in the new administration and 2) to stave off any chance of Hezbollah's success in the elections scheduled for June 7, so as not to alienate U.S. allies in Lebanon. In the meeting, Feltman raises the issues of Syria's support for terrorism, non-proliferation, intervention in Lebanese politics, and disintegrating human rights standards. After the meeting, Feltman is referred to as too "neo-con" by both Syrian officials and domestic media to be considered an effective negotiator.[363]

Mid-February 2009   Senator Kerry visits Bashar al-Assad in Damascus.[364] In preparation for his arrival, FM Spokesperson Bushra Kanafani said, "Senator Kerry, like the rest of U.S. delegates arriving in Damascus, is so welcome...We have always called for deep dialogue with Washington to put our relations on the right track, which would serve bilateral interests, security and stability."[365]

March 7, 2009   Feltman and Shapiro go to Syria in the highest level visit since 2005 to explore Washington's relationship with Damascus.[366] The two provided few specifics about the visit, but they said that the talks "constructive" and that they found "a lot of common ground" (in Feltman's words, es-

[361]Tabler, *In the Lion's Den*, 219

[362]Sharp, "Syria: Background and U.S. Relations," 2-3.

[363]Tabler, *In the Lion's Den*, 222.

[364]Heather Saul, "Pictures resurface showing US Secretary John Kerry and President Assad dining in Syria together," *The Independent,* September 3, 2013, http://www.independent.co.uk/news/world/middle-east/pictures-resurface-showing-us-secretary-john-kerry-and-president-assad-dining-in-syria-together-8796846.html.

[365]George Baghdadi, "John Kerry to Visit Syrian Capital," *CBS News,* February 12, 2009, http://www.cbsnews.com/news/john-kerry-to-visit-syrian-capital/.

[366]Elise Labott, "U.S., Syria find 'common ground' in diplomatic talks," *CNN,* March 7, 2009, http://edition.cnn.com/2009/WORLD/meast/03/07/US.Syria/index.html?eref=edition.

pecially on wanting a "unified Iraq").[367] Instead of setting "benchmarks" for Syria, Feltman and Shapiro say they are looking forward to each country watching the "choices" of the other.[368]

March 9, 2009   Assad begins to speaks publicly; in the following days he offers Israel a "cold peace" and announces he had been asked to mediate between the U.S. and Iran. He demanded U.S. mediation for the Arab-Israeli conflict and requested direct contact with President Obama.[369]

May 7, 2009   According to Feltman, Feltman and Shapiro revisit Syria "as part of President Obama's commitments to use diplomacy and to use dialogue in order to try to see where we can move forward, where our interests overlap, and to see where we can try and work together to bridge the difference that remain in some of our policies." Feltman recognizes improvements in the bilateral relationship compared to two months ago.[370] Also this day, the Obama administration, in accordance with the National Emergencies Act, renews the annual iteration of a National Emergency with respect to Syria. The declaration allows the administration to continue targeted sanctions on government and security officials.[371]

June 8, 2009   Obama gives the famous "Cairo Speech" in which he charts a new course for U.S.-Middle East relations, promising characterizes his Middle East policy as centered around the Middle East Peace Process and U.S. withdrawal from Iraq.[372]

June 13, 2009   U.S. Envoy George Mitchell and Jeff Feltman visit Damascus in the highest level visit since 2005.[373] He announces that Syria is critical for a comprehensive Middle East Peace: "Syria has an integral role to play in reaching comprehensive peace," Mr. Mitchell said. Both Syria and the United States

---

[367]See Sharp, "Syria: Background and U.S. Relations, 2.)

[368]Tabler, *In the Lion's Den*, 222.

[369]Tabler, *In the Lion's Den*, 222-223.

[370]Sharp, "Syria: Background and U.S. Relations," 3-4.

[371]Sharp, "Syria: Background and U.S. Relations," 4.

[372]Barack Obama, "Remarks By The President On A New Beginning," Press Release, June 4, 2009 (online by the White House Office of the Press Secretary), http://www.whitehouse.gov/the_press_office/Remarks-by-the-President-at-Cairo-University-6-04-09.

[373]"Mitchell Cites Syria's Role in Mideast Peace Effort," *The New York Times*, June 13, 2009, http://www.nytimes.com/2009/06/14/world/middleeast/14mitchell.html?_r=0.

have the responsibility "to create conditions for negotiations to begin promptly and end successfully." He also offered, "It's my hope that we can also see full diplomatic relations and friendship restored between Damascus and Washington at an early day in the New Year."[374] Days after the visit, the U.S. declares it will reinstate its ambassador.[375]

Late June 2009   The administration sends Ambassador Hof and a delegation from CENTCOM in June and August 2009 to discuss cutting off the flow of foreign fighters and to assess Syria's border-monitoring will and capacity.[376]

Late June 2009   The Obama administration messages that it plans to return an ambassador to the Syrian capital within the next few months.[377] Senator Kerry is reportedly very supportive of this move.[378]

July 26, 2009   U.S. Envoy Mitchell visits Syria in a further demonstration of thawing U.S.-Syrian relations.[379] Mitchell apparently spent hours with Assad personally reviewing U.S. sanctions after the head of state reiterated its demand that the U.S. pullback its economic pressure.[380] Mitchell called on the Arab world to begin normalization efforts with Israel. Syria said it was "looking forward" to the visit as "the first step of dialogue. He also mentioned that the U.S. was "trying to develop...bilateral issues that we have with the Syrians as well" and that they would discuss those issues at the meeting. Finally, Sen. Mitchell said, "In terms of the Syrian-American relationship, the United States is committed to a dialogue based on mutual interest and mutual respect and a solid foundation for discussion of our shared goals and of real differences, where they occur."[381]

[374]George Baghdadi, "Syria Hopes for "Natural Relations" with U.S.," *CBS News,* June 13, 2009, http://www.cbsnews.com/news/syria-hopes-for-natural-relations-with-us/.

[375]Tabler, *In the Lion's Den*, 223.

[376]Sharp, "Syria: Background and U.S. Relations," 4.

[377]Ibid.

[378]Heather Saul, "Pictures resurface showing US Secretary John Kerry and President Assad dining in Syria together," *The Independent,* September 3, 2013, http://www.independent.co.uk/news/world/middle-east/pictures-resurface-showing-us-secretary-john-kerry-and-president-assad-dining-in-syria-together-8796846.html.

[379]Josef Ferman, "George Mitchell In Syria: Obama Determined To See "Truly Comprehensive" Mideast Peace," *The Huffington Post,* August 26, 2009, http://www.huffingtonpost.com/2009/07/26/george-mitchell-in-syria-_n_245019.html.

[380]Tabler, *In the Lion's Den,* 223.

[381]"Obama's Middle East Envoy Steps Up Diplomatic Push in Syria."

July 28, 2009	The United States takes steps to ease sanctions on Syria, especially on sectors involving information technology (IT), civil aviation, and communications.[382]
July 30, 2009	Obama extends his presidential authority to enforce EO 13441 that freezing assets of anyone who tries to undermine Lebanon's sovereignty by reissuing a "continuation of National Emergency with Respect to Actions of Certain Persons to Undermine the Sovereignty of Lebanon or its Democratic Processes and Institutions."[383]
Early/Mid-August 2009	Another CENTCOM delegation visits Damascus and announces that the U.S. will form a tripartite committee with Iraq and Syria to ensure greater border security.[384]
August 19, 2009	After a visit to Damascus, Iraqi PM al-Maliki is almost blown up in Baghdad. Iraq accused Syria of hosting terrorist camps, which it said were responsible for the attacks.[385] Iraq withdrew its ambassador and engagement. The tripartite security agreement is now dead in the water.[386]
Late September 2009	Deputy Foreign Minister Faisal al-Miqdad is invited to Washington for high-level talks, almost exclusively on sanctions.[387] This is the first visit by a Syrian official to the U.S. in more than 8 years.[388] FM Walid Moallem declares, "I am optimistic about this visit...the agenda is clear; it is continuing the Syrian-U.S. dialogue to normalize bilateral relations. There are, of course, many obstacles and suspicions after an eight-year suspension of contacts. The gap must be bridged...This is a continuing process and this is part of the dialogue."[389] However, Syria shows little to no flexibility in its foreign policy—it continues its support of U.S.-designated terrorists, refuses to engage in rapprochement with Israel, and continues its repressive human rights record.

[382]"Syria's Response to US Engagement," Lebanese Information Center, Fact Sheet, March 15, 2010, http://www.licus.org/liclib/2010-04-19%20LIC%20FACT%20SHEET-SYRIA's%20 RESPONSE%20TO%20US%20ENGAGEMEN.pdf.

[383]Sharp, "Syria: Background and U.S. Relations," 4.

[384]Tabler, "Syria Clenches Its Fist."

[385]Sharp, "Syria: Background and U.S. Relations," 5.

[386]Tabler, *In the Lion's Den,* 226.

[387]Ibid; See also "Syria's Response to US Engagement," Lebanese Information Center, March 15, 2010, http://www.licus.org/liclib/2010-04-19%20LIC%20FACT%20SHEET-SYRIA's%20 RESPONSE%20TO%20US%20ENGAGEMEN.pdf.

[388]Sharp, "Syria: Background and U.S. Relations," 5.

[389]Ibid.

November 2009	Israel seizes a freighter from Iran to Syrian port of Latakia that is loaded with arms (medium range 107-mm and 122-mm rockets, armor piercing rounds, grenades, Kalashnikov ammunition); it is believed to be destined for use by Hezbollah in Lebanon.[390]
December 2009	U.S. denies Airbus the ability to sell Syria planes, as Airbus planes are approximately 40% U.S. origin, making them illegal to sell without an export license.
February 16, 2010	This week, amid growing U.S. pressure for a peace settlement, a "war of words" is exchanged between Syria and Israel after Ehud Barak told the Israeli Defense Forces, that "in the absence of an arrangement with Syria, we are liable to enter a belligerent clash with it that could reach the point of an all-out, regional war...just like the familiar reality in the Middle East, we will immediately sit down [with Syria] after such a war and negotiate on the exact same issues which we have been discussing with them for the last 15 years." While Barak likely meant it as a way to push Israeli citizens to favor negotiations, Syrian officials responded to the threat of war. Moallem responded, "Israel knows that if it declares war on Syria, such a war will reach its cities."[391]
February 17, 2010	Deputy Secretary of State William Burns meets with Bashar al-Assad.[392] The same day, the President announces that Robert Ford will be his choice for Ambassador to Syria.[393] Allegedly, the U.S. and Syria held additional talks soon after to discuss weapons smuggling to Hezbollah through Syria.[394]
February 18, 2010	U.S. Counterterrorism official Daniel Benjamin meets with Syrian Deputy FM al-Miqdad and is accompanied by a surprise guest, Gen. Ali Mamlouk, head of Syria's General Intelligence Directorate.[395] The group discusses possible areas of cooperation for counterterrorism.

[390]Charles S. Levinson and Josh Mitnick, "Israeli Navy Seizes Weapons Believed to Be for Hezbollah," *The Wall Street Journal*, November 5, 2009, http://www.wsj.com/news/articles/SB125732536158927651.

[391]"Believe in Israel, Believe in Peace," Americans for Peace Now, *Middle East Peace Report* 11, No. 18 (February 16, 2010): http://archive.peacenow.org/entries/peace_report_february_16_2010.

[392]"Top US William Burns Envoy in Syria for Talks," *BBC News*, February 17, 2010, http://news.bbc.co.uk/2/hi/middle_east/8520917.stm.

[393]Tabler, *In the Lion's Den*, 228.

[394]Sharp, "Syria: Background and U.S. Relations," 6.

[395]"US embassy cables: Syrian spy chief's surprise appearance at US talks," *The Guardian*, December 6, 2010, http://www.theguardian.com/world/us-embassy-cables-documents/250462.

February 20, 2010   Syria buys two French airplanes after discussions between France and Syria. It does not violate U.S. sanctions law, but the deal was financed by the Commercial Bank of Syria, which goes around Section 311 of the PATRIOT Act that forbids U.S. financial institutions' ability to work with the CBS.[396]

February 2010   The IAEA reports that Syria may have been involved in a nuclear program at the al-Kibar facility given the level of uranium particles found in the soil. Previous reports had declared that the uranium was not from Syria's declared inventory.[397]

February 24, 2010   Clinton tells a Senate committee that the United States was "asking Syria to move away from Iran."[398]

February 25, 2010   Yet the next day, at what is referred to as the "Axis of Evil Banquet" among Syria, Iran, and Hezbollah, Ahmadinejad and Assad defiantly mock Clinton's request, saying "there is no distance between Iran and Syria..."[399]

Early March 2010   Syria criticizes the Arab League for approving of proximity talks between Israel and the Palestinian Authority. Syrian officials argued that the move was a way for the Arab League to cover for the decision that the PA had already made.[400]

March 2010   A 2010 Human Rights Watch report condemned U.S. foreign policy relations with Syria saying it encouraged bad behavior on the part of the government: "[T]alking to Syria without putting its rights record on the table emboldens the government to believe that it can do whatever it wants to its people, without consequence," and that A message to Syria that says 'We only care about your external affairs' is a green light for repression."

March 16, 2010   At Robert Ford's nomination hearing, the Ambassador-Designate outlines 5 key issue areas in the U.S.-Syrian bilateral relationship: 1) Syria's help in stabilizing Iraq, 2) stability in Lebanon, 3) Syria's support for talks with Israel, 4) Syria's cooperation with the IAEA, and 5) an improvement in the human rights situation. Sanctions would not be lifted, Ford says, if these are not addressed.[401] Ford said of Syria: "Without significant changes in its policy, Syria

---

[396]Sharp, "Syria: Background and U.S. Relations," 6.

[397]Ibid.

[398]Tabler, *In the Lion's Den*, 228–229.

[399]Ibid.

[400]Sharp, "Syria: Background and U.S. Relations," 7.

[401]Tabler, "How to React to a Reactor."

will remain on our list of State Sponsors of Terrorism for the foreseeable future. And while we and our friends in the region are working to mitigate Iran's influence, Syria has helped promote Iran's destabilizing policies...I do not think that the Syrians will change their policies quickly. Finding avenues of cooperation with Syria will be a step-by-step process that will require patience and steady commitment to our principles."[402]

March 31, 2010   Sen. Kerry visits Syria.

Early April 2010   Syria allegedly transfers Scud missiles to Hezbollah, though Syria denies the accusations.[403] The missiles they sent are thought to have the capability to carry chemical warheads, though there is no evidence that Hezbollah has chemical weapons. The State Department says that it condemns the weapons transfer.[404]

April 21, 2010   Feltman testifies before the House Foreign Affairs Committee, Subcommittee on Middle East and South Asia, announcing that the administration plans to send Ambassador Ford to Damascus upon confirmation from the Senate. Feltman states, "As we try to minimize the prospects of war and maximize the chances for peace in a region where our national security is defended by American men and women in uniform, we have no choice but to use all the tools of statecraft at our disposal. We simply must make sure that leaders in Syria and elsewhere understand fully and accurately the position of the U.S. before they act - this is not something to be left to rumor, to second- or third-hand knowledge, or to others. This is our job. To do less amounts to negligence; to unilateral diplomatic disarmament. This is not the option we will pursue."[405]

April 22, 2010   Clinton states, "The larger question as to what the United States will do with respect to Syria is one we've spent a lot of time considering and debating inside the administration... Where we are as of today is that we believe it is important to continue the process to return an ambassador; this is not some kind of reward for the Syrians and the actions they take that are deeply disturbing."[406]

[402]Sharp, "Syria: Background and U.S. Relations," 7.

[403]Mark Landler, "U.S. Speaks to Syrian Envoy of Arms Worries," *The New York Times,* April 19, 2010, http://www.nytimes.com/2010/04/20/world/middleeast/20syria.html?_r=0.

[404]Sharp, "Syria: Background and U.S. Relations," 8.

[405]Ibid.

[406]Ibid.

September 16, 2010	U.S. Envoy George Mitchell visits Syria again in order to persuade it to back Israeli-Palestinian peace talks, but the Golan Heights issue and the seize on the Gaza strip seem to hamper progress.[407]
January 16, 2011	The United States appoints an ambassador to Syria after withdrawing its chief diplomat in 2005 over suspicions of Syrian involvement in the assassination of Lebanese president Rafik Hariri.[408]
January 31, 2011	In an interview with WSJ, Assad says Syria is immune to the type of violence shaking North Africa because the regime is "very closely linked to the beliefs of the people."[409]
March 16, 2011	Senator John Kerry makes a statement at the Carnegie Endowment, claiming that he believed Assad would reform and engage more meaningfully with the U.S. and its allies: "[M]y judgment is that Syria will move; Syria will change, as it embraces a legitimate relationship with the United States and the West and economic opportunity that comes with it and the participation that comes with it."[410] By this point in time, he had met with Assad six times in two years. Soon after, he makes this statement: "President Assad has been very generous with me in terms of the discussions we have had," he said after his March speech. "And when I last went to – the last several trips to Syria – I asked President Assad to do certain things to build the relationship with the United States and sort of show the good faith that would help us to move the process forward...So my judgment is that Syria will move; Syria will change, as it embraces a legitimate relationship with the United States and the West and economic opportunity that comes with it and the participation that comes with it."[411]

---

[407]Sarah Birke and Borzou Daragahi, "U.S. envoy Mitchell meets with Syrian president," *Los Angeles Times*, September 17, 2010, http://articles.latimes.com/2010/sep/17/world/la-fg-mitchell-syria-20100917.

[408]"First US ambassador for six years takes up post in Syria," *The Guardian*, January 16, 2011, http://www.theguardian.com/world/2011/jan/16/new-us-ambassador-syria.

[409]"Interview With Syrian President Bashar al-Assad," *The Wall Street Journal*, January 31, 2011, http://www.wsj.com/news/articles/SB10001424052748703833204576114712441122894.

[410]John Kerry, "Senator John Kerry on U.S Policy Toward the Middle East" (speech at the Carnegie Endowment for International Peace, Washington, DC, March 16, 2011), http://carnegieendowment.org/files/0317carnegie-johnkerry.pdf. ; Rogin, "Kerry: It's time to give up on Assad the reformer."

[411]Harriet Alexander, "John Kerry and Bashar al-Assad dined in Damascus," *The Telegraph*, September 3, 2013, http://www.telegraph.co.uk/news/worldnews/middleeast/syria/10283045/John-Kerry-and-Bashar-al-Assad-dined-in-Damascus.html.

March 27, 2011	Sec. Clinton makes comments on "Face the Nation" that Assad is a reformer, confirming Sen. Kerry's earlier portrayal of the U.S. position. Sec. Clinton received a lot of criticism for her characterization of the Middle East leader.[412]
March 30, 2011	Assad delivers a speech to the Syrian parliament that puts a nail in the coffin of "Assad the Reformer."[413] His defiant, conspiratorial speech signals to the Obama administration that Assad may no longer be a man with whom it could negotiate.[414]
April 8, 2011	Pres. Obama issues a statement condemning the violence and calling the regime to address the "legitimate aspirations" of the people.[415]
April 22, 2011	Pres. Obama issues a statement condemning the violence at the hand of the regime in Hama. The White House says, "We call on President Assad to change course now, and heed the calls of his own people."[416]
April 29, 2011	Pres. Obama signs Executive Order 13572 that declares the regime's "continuing escalation of violence against the people" a national emergency.[417] It imposes targeted sanctions on individuals and entities such as President Assad's brother Maher as well as the Iranian Revolutionary Guard Corps-Quds Force (IRGC-QF). The Dept. of Commerce revokes commercial export licenses pertaining to Syrian official VIP aircrafts. In her first official comments on the crisis, Sec. of State Clinton issues a press statement regarding the Human Rights Council's Special Session on Syria. She applauds the resolution put forth by the UNHRC that condemns human rights abuses by the regime and encourages the establishment of an urgent investigation into those abuses.[418]

[412]Glenn Kessler, "Hillary Clinton's uncredible statement on Syria," *The Washington Post*, April 4, 2011, http://www.washingtonpost.com/blogs/fact-checker/post/hillary-clintons-uncredible-statement-on-syria/2011/04/01/AFWPEYaC_blog.html.

[413]Bashar al-Assad, "Syria: speech by Bashar al-Assad" (speech to the Syrian parliament, Syria, March 30, 2011), http://www.al-bab.com/arab/docs/syria/bashar_assad_speech_110330.htm.

[414]Fred Hof, Interview

[415]Barack Obama, "Statement from the President on the Violence in Syria," Press Release, April 8, 2011 (online by the White House Office of the Press Secretary), http://www.whitehouse.gov/the-press-office/2011/04/08/statement-president-violence-syria.

[416]Schulman, "A Statement by President Obama on Syria."

[417]"Fact Sheet on Syria," Press Release, August 18, 2011 (online by the White House Office of the Press Secretary), http://www.whitehouse.gov/the-press-office/2011/08/18/fact-sheet-syria.

[418]Hillary Rodham Clinton, "The Human Rights Council's Special Session on Syria," Press Release, April 29, 2011 (online by Department of State), http://www.state.gov/secretary/20092013clinton/rm/2011/04/162260.htm.

May 6, 2011	Sec. Clinton condemns "in the strongest terms" the repressive tactics of the Assad regime and endorses the right of the Syrian people to exercise the freedom of speech.[419]
May 10, 2011	Sen. Kerry states that there is no more hope for "Assad the Reformer": "He obviously is not a reformer now...I've always said the top goal of Assad is to perpetuate his own regime."[420]
May 11, 2011	Syria withdraws its candidacy for the UN Human Rights Council after aggressive U.S. lobbying to prevent is accession to the UN body.[421]
May 18, 2011	Pres. Obama issues Executive Order 13573 that imposes targeted sanctions on Assad and other key Syrian officials for human rights abuses.[422] The Dept. of Commerce also suspends specific licenses related to Syria's Boeing 747 aircrafts.
May 19, 2011	Pres. Obama gives his famous "Middle East Speech" in response to developments in the Arab Spring. Obama condemns Assad's violent response, realistically assessing that "President Assad now has a choice: he can lead that transition, or get out of the way."[423]
May 25, 2011	George Mitchell visits Syria again to demonstrate Pres. Obama's commitment to a comprehensive Middle East Peace, saying he welcomed "the full cooperation of the Syrian Arab Republic in this historic endeavor." [424]
June 15, 2011	The United States and Canada draft a statement signed by 54 UN member states that addresses the deteriorating human rights situation in Syria and urges the Syrian government to allow access to the UN High Commissioner for Human Rights' fact-finding mission.[425]

[419]Hillary Rodham Clinton, "Violence in Syria," Press Release, May 6, 2011 (online by Department of State), http://www.state.gov/secretary/20092013clinton/rm/2011/05/162843.htm.

[420]Rogin, "Kerry: It's Time to Give up on Assad the Reformer."

[421]"Fact Sheet on Syria."

[422]"Fact Sheet on Syria."; Arshad Mohammed and Khaled Yacoub Oweis, "U.S. imposes sanctions on Syria's Assad," Reuters, May 18, 2011, http://www.reuters.com/article/2011/05/18/us-syria-idUSLDE73N02P20110518.

[423]Rogin, "Full Text of Obama's Middle East Speech."

[424]Josef Federman, "George Mitchell In Syria: Obama Determined To See "Truly Comprehensive" Mideast Peace," Huffington Post, August 26, 2009, http://www.huffingtonpost.com/2009/07/26/george-mitchell-in-syria-_n_245019.html.

[425]"Fact Sheet on Syria."

June 20, 2011:   Assad gives a speech at Damascus University, Assad blames the protests on "conspirators" and "takfiri elements" more so than on the legitimate concerns of the Syrian people.[426]

July 1, 2011   Sec. Clinton says that there must be a "genuine transition to democracy" in Syria and that the "Syrian Government is running out of time" to allow for a more inclusive political process.[427]

July 8, 2011   Ambassador Robert Ford makes his famous trip to Hama, where protestors view his presence as a force of protection, sure that the government would not act with him there.[428] The Treasury Department issues a warning to U.S. financial institutions alerting them to the potential for increased illicit financial activities involving accounts held by or on behalf of senior political figures in Syria, as a result of the unrest in Syria.[429]

July 11, 2011   Sec. Clinton says that Assad has lost legitimacy and that he should not consider himself "indispensable" to Syria's future.[430]

July 15, 2011   Sec. Clinton reiterates that "Assad has lost legitimacy" and that the U.S. supports a democratic transition in Syria; however the future of Syria lies in the hands of Syrians themselves.[431]

July 22, 2011   The State Dept. imposes travel restrictions on the Syrian Embassy in Washington, D.C., in response to Syrian efforts to restrict the movement of U.S. diplomats in Damascus. Syrian diplomats now must request permission prior to leaving Washington, D.C.[432]

August 10, 2011   U.S. Treasury freezes assets of the Commercial Bank of Syria as the bank was linked to suspicious weapons deals.[433]

---

[426]"Highlights: Syrian President Bashar al-Assad's speech on unrest," *Reuters,* June 20, 2011, http://www.reuters.com/article/2011/06/20/us-syria-assad-speech-idUSTRE75J1U720110620.

[427]Hillary Rodham Clinton, "Remarks on Syria," Press Release, July 1, 2011 (online by Department of State), http://www.state.gov/secretary/20092013clinton/rm/2011/07/167502.htm.

[428]"Robert Ford, U.S. Ambassador To Syria, Causes Controversy With Visit To Hama," *The Huffington Post,* July 8, 2011, http://www.huffingtonpost.com/2011/07/08/robert-ford-us-ambassador_n_893522.html.

[429]"Fact Sheet on Syria."

[430]"Clinton Says Syria's Assad 'Not Indispensable.'"

[431]Hillary Rodham Clinton, "Remarks on Libya and Syria," Press Release, July 15, 2011(online by Department of State), http://www.state.gov/secretary/20092013clinton/rm/2011/07/168656.htm.

[432]"Fact Sheet on Syria."

[433]Jeff Bliss, "U.S. Treasury to Freeze Assets of Syrian Bank," *Bloomberg,* August 10, 2011, http://www.bloomberg.com/news/2011-08-10/u-s-treasury-to-freeze-assets-of-syrian-bank.html.

August 12, 2011	Sec. Clinton says, "There are Syrian opposition figures outside of Syria and inside. But there's no address for the opposition. There is no place for any of us who wish to assist can go."[434]
August 18, 2011	Pres. Obama asserts, "The future of Syria must be determined by its people...Assad must step aside."[435] Additionally, Pres. Obama issues an executive order that imposes the harshest petroleum sanctions the government had taken thus far. Targeted sanctions have been imposed on 32 Syrian and Iranian individuals.[436]
August 23, 2011	Sec. Clinton congratulates the Human Rights Council for the establishment of an independent Commission of Inquiry to investigate human rights abuses in Syria. She echoes Pres. Obama's call for Assad to step aside "for the sake of the Syrian people."[437]
October 5, 2011	Amb. Susan Rice storms out of a UN Security Council meeting after China and Russia exercise a double veto, the first since 2008, to turn down a resolution that would condemn Assad's violence in Syria.[438]
October 24, 2011	U.S. withdraws Ambassador Robert Ford from Syria due to security concerns.[439]
November 12, 2011	Sec. Clinton says that the Arab League's decision to suspend Syria demonstrates that "the international pressure will continue to build until the brutal Asad regime heeds the calls of its own people."[440]

[434]"Hillary Clinton urges countries to cut energy, arms ties with Syria,"*Al Arabiya News,* August 12, 2011, http://www.alarabiya.net/articles/2011/08/12/161919.html.

[435]Barack Obama, "Statement by President Obama on the Situation in Syria," Press Release, August 18, 2011 (online by the White House Office of the Press Secretary), http://www.whitehouse.gov/the-press-office/2011/08/18/statement-president-obama-situation-syria.

[436]"Fact Sheet on Syria."

[437]Hillary Rodham Clinton, "The Human Rights Council's Special Session on Syria," Press Release, April 23, 2011 (online by U.S. Department of State), http://www.state.gov/secretary/20092013clinton/rm/2011/08/170949.htm.

[438]Daniel Miller, "'They'd rather sell arms than stand with the Syrian people': U.S. envoy storms out after Russia and China veto U.N resolution," *Daily Mail,* October 5, 2011, http://www.dailymail.co.uk/news/article-2045442/US-envoy-Susan-Rice-storms-Russia-China-veto-UN-resolution.html.

[439]MacAskill, "US pulls ambassador Robert Ford out of Syria over security concerns."

[440]Hillary Rodham Clinton, "Arab League Suspends Syria," Remarks, November 12, 2011 (online by U.S. Department of State), http://www.state.gov/secretary/20092013clinton/rm/2011/11/177044.htm.

December 2, 2011   In a press statement, Sec. Clinton lauds the work by the Human Rights Council to further the isolation of the Syrian government and draw attention to its abuses by endorsing a report issued by the independent International Commission of Inquiry on Syria.[441] VP Biden visits neighboring Turkey to discuss options on Syria and Iran.[442]

December 6, 2011   At a meeting with the Syrian National Council in Geneva, Sec. Clinton emphasizes the importance of creating an inclusive, post-Assad Syrian government.[443]

January 30, 2012   Sec. Clinton condemns the sharp escalation in regime brutality against its people and encourages the UNSC to make clear the threat that the Syrian regime poses to international peace and security.[444]

January 31, 2012   Sec. Clinton speaks at the UN confirming U.S. commitment to reaching a resolution on ending the conflict in Syria and lauding the Arab League for its involvement and support.[445] She also calls Libya a "false analogy" for UNSC involvement.[446]

February 4, 2012   Pres. Obama issues a statement commemorating the thirty-year anniversary of the Hama Massacre and condemning the ongoing violence under the Assad regime.[447]

[441]Hillary Rodham Clinton, "The Human Rights Council's Special Session on Syria," Remarks, December 2, 2011 (online by U.S. Department of State) http://www.state.gov/secretary/20092013clinton/rm/2011/12/178137.htm.

[442]Mark Landler, "In Turkey, Biden Talks About Iran and Syria," *The New York Times,* December 2, 2011, http://www.nytimes.com/2011/12/03/world/middleeast/biden-confers-with-turkish-leaders-about-syria-and-iran.html?_r=0.

[443]Hillary Rodham Clinton, "Remarks at Meeting with Syrian National Council," Remarks, December 6, 2011(online by U.S. Department of State), http://www.state.gov/secretary/20092013clinton/rm/2011/12/178332.htm.

[444]Hillary Rodham Clinton, "Sharp Escalation of Regime Violence in Syria," Press Release, January 30, 2012 (online by U.S. Department of State), http://www.state.gov/secretary/20092013clinton/rm/2012/01/182720.htm.

[445]Hillary Rodham Clinton, "Remarks Following UNSC Meeting on Syria," Remarks, January 31, 2012 (online by U.S. Department of State), http://www.state.gov/secretary/20092013clinton/rm/2012/01/182848.htm.

[446]Hillary Rodham Clinton, "Remarks at a United Nations Security Council Session on the Situation in Syria," Remarks, January 31, 2012 (online by U.S. Department of State), http://www.state.gov/secretary/20092013clinton/rm/2012/01/182845.htm.

[447]Barack Obama, "Statement by the President on Syria," Press Release, February 4, 2012 (online by the White House Office of the Press Secretary), http://www.whitehouse.gov/the-press-office/2012/02/04/statement-president-syria.

February 5, 2012	Russia and China veto a UN Security Council Resolution that would have formally condemned Assad for the violence in Syria. Amb. Susan Rice deems the double veto "outrageous" and disgusting.[448]
February 8, 2012	Sens. John McCain, Lindsay Graham, and Joe Lieberman issue a statement declaring that the Obama administration should consider providing arms to the Syrian opposition.[449]
February 6, 2012	U.S. Embassy in Damascus suspends operations.[450]
February 24, 2012	In Tunis, at the first-ever Friend of Syrian People meeting, Sec. Clinton echoes the Arab League's demand for a halt to violence against civilians, calls for the negotiated political solution to the crisis, and confirms U.S. commitment to the sovereignty of Syria.[451] She also calls Russia and China's repeated use of the veto power in the UNSC "despicable" when people are being murdered.[452]
February 26, 2012	In an interview with CBS in Rabat, Sec. Clinton made comments backpedalling slightly on U.S. involvement in Syria, asking "I'm wondering is what about the people in Damascus, what about the people in Aleppo? Don't they know that their fellow Syrian men, women, and children are being slaughtered by their government?...When are they going to start pulling the props out from under this illegitimate regime?" In an answer to a question as to when the threshold for violence will warrant international intervention, Sec. Clinton responded, "If you take just a moment to imagine all the terrible conflicts that go on in the world, we have seen in the last 15 years millions of people killed in the Eastern Congo in the most brutal, terrible, despicable ways. It wasn't on TV. There were no Skype-ing from the jungles that were the killing fields.

[448]"Syria Veto 'Outrageous' Says U.N. Envoy Susan Rice," *NPR*, February 5, 2012, http://www.npr.org/2012/02/05/146424981/un-ambassador-susan-rice-fumes-at-syria-veto.

[449]"Graham, McCain, Lieberman Statement on Syria."

[450]Att Spetalnick and Andrew Quinn, "U.S. closes embassy in Syria, vows further pressure," *Reuters*, February 6, 2012, http://www.reuters.com/article/2012/02/06/us-syria-usa-embassy-idUSTRE81512C20120206.

[451]Hillary Rodham Clinton, "Intervention at the Friends of Syrian People Meeting," Press Release, February 24, 2012 (online by U.S. Department of State), http://www.state.gov/secretary/20092013clinton/rm/2012/02/184606.htm.

[452]Hillary Rodham Clinton, "the Meeting of the Friends of the Syrian People Press Availability on the Meeting of the Friends of the Syrian People," Press Release, February 24, 2012 (online by U.S. Department of State), http://www.state.gov/secretary/20092013clinton/rm/2012/02/184635.htm.

And I could point to many other places where governments oppress people, where governments are turning against their own people. And you have to be very clear-eyed about what is possible and what the consequences of anything you might wish to do could be. I am incredibly sympathetic to the calls that somebody do something. But it is also important to stop and ask what that is and who's going to do it and how capable anybody is of doing it. And I like to get to the second, third, and fourth order questions, and those are very difficult ones."[453]

March 29, 2012   Congress passes the National Defense Authorization Act for 2013. Among other things, the act requires the Secretary of Defense to report to the defense and appropriations committees identifying the limited military activities that could deny or significantly degrade the ability of President Bashar al-Assad of Syria and forces loyal to him to use air power against civilians and opposition groups in Syria. It also requires the Secretary to report to the defense and foreign relations committees on military assistance provided to Syria by the Russian Federation. The President signs it into effect on January 2, 2013.[454]

March 23, 2012   Syrians currently residing in the U.S. are granted Temporary Protected Status by Sec. of Homeland Security Janet Napolitano.

April 1, 2012   Friends of Syria Group meets for the second time.[455] Sec. Clinton makes a statement in Istanbul that the U.S. has "ratcheted up" its involvement in the crisis by introducing new sanctions on the regime, working with international partners to establish accountability measures, and increasing its humanitarian support, announcing an additional $12 million, bringing the U.S. contribution to $25 million.[456]

April 19, 2012   Sec. Clinton makes remarks in Paris at the Ad Hoc Ministerial Meeting on Syria supporting the monitoring mission

---

[453]Hillary Rodham Clinton, interview by Wyatt Andrews, *CBS,* February 26, 2012, http://www.state.gov/secretary/20092013clinton/rm/2012/02/184662.htm.

[454]*National Defense Authorization Act for Fiscal Year 2013*, HR 4310, 112th Congress, 2013, https://www.govtrack.us/congress/bills/112/hr4310.

[455]"The Second Conference of the Group of Friends of the Syrian People will take place in İstanbul," Republic of Turkey, Ministry of Foreign Affairs, http://www.mfa.gov.tr/the-second-conference-of-the-group-of-friends-of-the-syrian-people-will-take-place-in-istanbul.en.mfa.

[456]Hillary Rodham Clinton, "Intervention to the Friends of the Syrian People," Remarks, April 1, 2012 (online by U.S. Department of State), http://www.state.gov/secretary/20092013clinton/rm/2012/04/187295.htm.

	and demanding a tougher stance on Assad, suggesting a move toward Chapter 7 UN sanctions resolution.[457] Sec. of Defense Panetta makes a statement before the House Armed Services Committee on Syria.[458] He outlines first the U.S. approach to Syria then draws analogies to the intervention in Libya to demonstrate the utility of this approach.
June 1, 2012	Sec. Clinton lauds the UN Human Rights Council's adoption of a resolution that calls for an investigation of the massacre in Houla the week prior. She repeats the call for Assad to step aside.[459]
June 6, 2012	Sec. of Treasury Tim Geithner speaks to the Friends of the Syrian People Sanctions Working Group endorsing sanctions and commending nations on their progress so far.[460] Clinton issues a press statement on behalf of Working Group that sanctions are working in putting pressure on Syrian officials for their human rights abuses.[461]
June 24, 2012	Sec. Clinton reaffirms strong U.S. support for its Turkish ally after the Syrian shoot down of a Turkish plane.[462]
June 30, 2012	Following a meeting of the Action Group on Syria in Geneva, Sec. Clinton announces U.S. support of Special Envoy Kofi Annan's six-point plan for a Syrian-led transition to democracy. She also makes comments regarding Russian and Chinese changes to the original document.[463]

[457]Hillary Rodham Clinton, "Remarks at the Ad Hoc Ministerial Meeting on Syria," Remarks, April 19, 2012 (online by U.S. Department of State), http://www.state.gov/secretary/20092013clinton/rm/2012/04/188147.htm.

[458]Leon E. Panetta, Testimony on Syria before the House Armed Services Committee, Hearing, April 19, 2012, Available online at: http://www.defense.gov/Speeches/Speech.aspx?SpeechID=1663.

[459]Hillary Rodham Clinton, "The Human Rights Council's Special Session on Syria," Press Release, June 1, 2012 (online by U.S. Department of State), http://www.state.gov/secretary/20092013clinton/rm/2012/06/191673.htm.

[460]Tim Geithner, "Remarks by Secretary Tim Geithner before the Friends of the Syrian People, International Working Group on Sanctions," Press Release, June 6, 2012 (online by U.S. Department of the Treasury), http://www.treasury.gov/press-center/press-releases/Pages/tg1602.aspx.

[461]Hillary Rodham Clinton, "Friends of the Syrian People Sanctions Working Group," Press Release, June 6, 2012 (online by U.S. Department of State), http://www.state.gov/secretary/20092013clinton/rm/2012/06/191874.htm.

[462]Hillary Rodham Clinton, "Syrian Shoot-Down of Turkish Aircraft," Remarks, June 24, 2012 (online by U.S. Department of State), http://www.state.gov/secretary/20092013clinton/rm/2012/06/193962.htm.

[463]Hillary Rodham Clinton, "Press Availability Following the Meeting of the Action Group on Syria," Remarks, June 30, 2012 (online by U.S. Department of State), http://www.state.gov/secretary/20092013clinton/rm/2012/06/194328.htm.

July 6, 2012	Sec. Clinton makes remarks during Friends of the Syria Ministerial Meeting in Paris lauding the Geneva meeting of the five permanent UNSC members and the Arab League in support of the transition.[464] Sec. Clinton also makes comments after the meeting announcing the creation of a plan for an inclusive, Syrian-led, democratic transition and recognizing the challenges of implementing it. In addition to reiterating U.S. commitment to sanctions and communication with the opposition, Sec. Clinton announces that the United States is pursuing a UNSC resolution that would impose sanctions under Chapter 7.[465]
August 2, 2012	Sec. Clinton thanks Special Envoy Kofi Annan for his service upon news of his resignation and confirms U.S. commitment to the transition framework he envisioned.[466]
August 11, 2012	Sec. of State Clinton says from Istanbul that has been made clear to the Assad regime the use of chemical weapons is a "red line for the world."[467] The first use of the "red line" language by an administration official was first used in July 2012.[468]
August 17, 2012	Sec. Clinton welcomes Lakhdar Brahimi's appointment as Joint Special Representative for Syria.[469]
August 20, 2012	In a press conference, Pres. Obama states, "We have been

[464]Hillary Rodham Clinton, "Remarks at the Friends of the Syrian People Ministerial Meeting," Remarks, July 6, 2012 (online by U.S. Department of State), http://www.state.gov/secretary/20092013clinton/rm/2012/07/194628.htm; "'Friends of Syria' push for tougher sanctions," *France 24*, July 7, 2012, http://www.france24.com/en/20120706-diplomacy-friends-syria-sanctions-transition-plan-assad-paris-usa-un-arab/.

[465]Hillary Rodham Clinton, "Press Availability Following the Friends of the Syrian People Ministerial Meeting," Press Release, July 6, 2012 (online by U.S. Department of State), http://www.state.gov/secretary/20092013clinton/rm/2012/07/194634.htm.

[466]Hillary Rodham Clinton, "Resignation of Kofi Annan as Joint Special Envoy for Syria," Press Release, August 2, 2012 (online by U.S. Department of State), http://www.state.gov/secretary/20092013clinton/rm/2012/08/196017.htm.

[467]Hillary Rodham Clinton, "Remarks on Syria: Questions and Answers Session," Remarks, August 11, 2012 (online by U.S. Department of State), http://www.state.gov/secretary/20092013clinton/rm/2012/08/196394.htm; "Hillary Clinton on Syria: use of chemical weapons is a red line – video," *The Guardian*, August 11, 2012, http://www.theguardian.com/world/video/2012/aug/11/hillary-clinton-syria-chemical-weapons-video.

[468]Claudette Roulo, "Little: Syrian Chemical Weapons Appear Secure," *Department of Defense News*, July 13, 2012, http://www.defense.gov/news/newsarticle.aspx?id=117118.

[469]Hillary Rodham Clinton, "Appointment of Lakhdar Brahimi as Joint Special Representative for Syria," Press Release, August 17, 2012 (online by U.S. Department of State), http://www.state.gov/secretary/20092013clinton/rm/2012/08/196676.htm.

very clear to the Assad regime, but also to other players on the ground, that a red line for us is we start seeing a whole bunch of chemical weapons moving around or being utilized. That would change my calculus. That would change my equation."[470]

September 13, 2012	U.S. Treasury designates Hezbollah chief Hassan Nasrallah and other Hezbollah figures as targets for financial sanctions.[471]
September 28, 2012	Sec. of Defense Leon Panetta says most caches of Syrian chemical weapons are secure, but there are a few that cannot be accounted for by U.S. intelligence.[472] Sec. Clinton makes remarks at the Ad Hoc Friends of the Syrian People Ministerial in New York in which she announces an additional $30 million in humanitarian aid from the U.S., bringing the total U.S. contribution to $130 million. She also announces an additional $15 million for nonlethal aid, bringing support for the unarmed opposition to $45 million.[473]
November 11, 2012	The United States issues a press statement congratulating representatives for forming the coalition but stopped short of recognizing the Coalition as a "government in exile" despite having spearheaded efforts to unite the opposition.[474]
December 3, 2012	The President again warns Assad over chemical weapons at the National Defense University: "If you make the tragic mistake of using these weapons, there where be consequences, and you

[470]Barack Obama, "Remarks by the President to the White House Press Corps," Press Release, August 20, 2012 (online by the White House Office of the Press Secretary), http://www.white-house.gov/the-press-office/2012/08/20/remarks-president-white-house-press-corps.

[471]Terry Atlas, "Hezbollah Chief Designated for U.S. Sanctions for Syria," *Bloomberg*, September 13, 2012, http://www.bloomberg.com/news/2012-09-13/hezbollah-chief-designated-for-u-s-sanctions-for-syria.html.

[472]Lolita Baldor, "Syria Chemical Weapons Moved, Defense Secretary Leon Panetta Says," *The Huffington Post*, September 28, 2012, http://www.huffingtonpost.com/2012/09/28/syr-ia-chemical-weapons-moved-panetta_n_1923159.html.

[473]Hillary Rodham Clinton, "Remarks at the Ad Hoc Friends of the Syrian People Ministerial," Press Release, September 28, 2012 (online by U.S. Department of State), http://www.state.gov/secretary/20092013clinton/rm/2012/09/198455.htm.

[474]"US declares support for united Syrian opposition," *Hurriyet Daily News*, January 5, 2015, http://www.hurriyetdailynews.com/us-declares-support-for-united-syrian-opposition.aspx?Page-ID=238&NID=34455&NewsCatID=359; "National Coalition for Syrian Revolutionary and Opposition Forces," The Carnegie Endowment for International Peace, http://carnegieendow-ment.org/syriaincrisis/?fa=50628.

will be held accountable," Obama says.[475] On the same day, Sec. Clinton assures reporters that the U.S. is "planning to take action" if Assad's regime launches a chemical attack.[476]

December 11, 2012   The U.S. joins fellow members of the Friends of Syria Group at its fourth conference in Morocco in recognizing the Syrian National Coalition as the sole legitimate representative of the Syrian people.[477]

January 29, 2013   Pres. Obama announces the delivery of $155 million in humanitarian aid to Syria, bringing total U.S. aid to $365 million.[478]

February 2, 2013   VP Biden calls Assad a "tyrant hellbent on clinging to power...and he must go."[479]

February 7, 2013   Sec. of Defense Leon Panetta and JCS Chairman Dempsey tell a congressional panel that they agree with preliminary plans drafted by Sec. Clinton and CIA Director Petraeus to provide arms to rebel groups.[480] In doing so, Sec. Panetta is the first Western senior official to publicly support arming rebels against Assad.

February 28, 2013   Sec. Kerry makes a speech from Rome at the Friends of Syria Meeting communicating that the U.S. believes the "best solu-

[475]Barack Obama, "Remarks by the President at the Nunn-Lugar Cooperative Threat Reduction Symposium," Press Release, December 3, 2012 (online by the White House Office of the Press Secretary), http://www.whitehouse.gov/the-press-office/2012/12/03/remarks-president-nunn-lugar-cooperative-threat-reduction-symposium.

[476]Hillary Rodham Clinton, "Video Remarks on Syria," Remarks, December 3, 2012 (online by U.S. Department of State), http://www.state.gov/secretary/20092013clinton/rm/2012/12/199997.htm.

[477]"'Friends of Syria' recognise opposition," Al Jazeera, December 12, 2012, http://www.aljazeera.com/news/middleeast/2012/12/201212124541767116.html; "US recognises Syria opposition coalition says Obama," BBC News, December 12, 2012, http://www.bbc.com/news/world-middle-east-20690148.

[478]Barack Obama, "Statement by the President Announcing $155 Million in Additional Humanitarian Assistance for the Syrian People," Press Release, January 29, 2013 (online by the White House Office of the Press Secretary), http://www.whitehouse.gov/the-press-office/2013/01/29/president-obama-announces-155-million-additional-humanitarian-aid-syrian.

[479]Patrick Donahue and Jonathan Tirone, "Biden Says Syria's Assad 'Hellbent' on Power, Must Go," Bloomberg, February 2, 2013, http://www.bloomberg.com/news/2013-02-01/syrian-opposition-may-seek-no-fly-zone-as-envoy-tells-un-to-lead.html.

[480]Jon Swaine, "Leon Panetta supports Hillary Clinton plan to arm Syrian rebels," The Telegraph, February 7, 2013, http://www.telegraph.co.uk/news/worldnews/middleeast/syria/9856382/Leon-Panetta-supports-Hillary-Clinton-plan-to-arm-Syrian-rebels.html.

tion for Syria is a political solution."[481] He also announces the donation of $60 million in nonlethal assistance.[482]

April 25, 2013 — U.S. and Britain demand an investigation into reports of governmental chemical weapons use.[483]

April 11, 2013 — In a presidential memorandum, Pres. Obama authorizes the drawdown of up to $10 million in the resources of "any agency" at the discretion of the Sec. of State and Congress so that the money may be provided as foreign assistance to the Syrian Opposition Coalition and the Supreme Military Command.[484]

April 17, 2013 — Sec. Kerry issues a press statement commemorating Syria National Day and extending his sympathies for the Syrians who struggle against Assad.[485] Sec. Hagel speaks at the Senate Armed Services Committee hearing advocating strongly for a political solution though he notes the military has prepared contingency plans. He states, "Military intervention is always an option...but one of last resort."[486]

April 21, 2013 — Sec. Kerry makes remarks with FM Ahmet Davutoğlu and Etilaf (SNC) Pres. Moaz al-Khatib after a meeting of the Friends of Syria in Istanbul laying out the opposition's vision for Syria's future.[487] Sec. Kerry outlines key concerns in Syria:

[481]John Kerry, "Press Availability on Syria," Remarks, February 28, 2013 (online by U.S. Department of State), http://www.state.gov/secretary/remarks/2013/02/205435.htm; Michael Mainville and Nicolas Revise, "US set to boost support for Syria opposition," *Middle East Online,* February 28, 2013, http://www.middle-east-online.com/english/?id=57241.

[482]John Kerry, "Remarks With Italian Foreign Minister Giulio Terzi and Syrian Opposition Council Chairman Moaz al-Khatib," Remarks, February 28, 2013 (online by U.S. Department of State), http://www.state.gov/secretary/remarks/2013/02/205457.htm.

[483]Michael Eisenstadt, "Investigating Alleged Chemical Weapons Use in Syria: Technical and Political Challenges," The Washington Institute, Policywatch 2072, April 26, 2013, http://www.washingtoninstitute.org/policy-analysis/view/investigating-alleged-chemical-weapons-use-in-syria-technical-and-political.

[484]Barack Obama, "Presidential Memorandum -- Presidential Determination on Syria Drawdown," Memorandum for the Secretary of State, The Secretary of Defense, April 11, 2013 (online by the White House Office of the Press Secretary), http://www.whitehouse.gov/the-press-office/2013/04/11/presidential-memorandum-presidential-determination-syria-drawdown.

[485]John Kerry, "Syria National Day Message," Press Release, April 17, 2013 (online by U.S. Department of State), http://www.state.gov/secretary/remarks/2013/04/207662.htm.

[486]Chuck Hagel, Statement before the Senate Armed Services Committee, Hearing, April 17, 2013, Available online at: http://www.defense.gov/Speeches/Speech.aspx?SpeechID=1771.

[487]John Kerry, "Remarks With Turkish Foreign Minister Ahmet Davutoglu and Syrian Opposition Coalition President Moaz al-Khatib," Remarks, April 21, 2013 (online by U.S. Department of State), http://www.state.gov/secretary/remarks/2013/04/207811.htm; Tulin Daloglu, "Friends of Syria Deliver Nothing New," *Al Monitor's Turkey Pulse,* April 21, 2013, http://www.al-monitor.com/pulse/originals/2013/04/syrian-opposition-radical-elements-wester-arms.html.

"chemical weapons; the slaughter of people by ballistic missiles and other weapons of huge destruction; the potential for the whole country...breaking up into enclaves; [and the] potential of sectarian violence."

April 25, 2013   The White House issues a letter to Congress stating that U.S. intelligence had reports that Assad had used chemical weapons twice so far against his own people, but reports were not solid enough to warrant U.S. involvement in the conflict.[488] Sec. Hagel reiterates these suspicions and says that the U.S. has an "obligation to investigate."[489]

May 1, 2013   Pres. Obama issues the executive order, "Prohibiting Certain Transactions with and Suspending Entry into the United States of Foreign Sanctions Evaders with respect to Iran and Syria." This order tightens sanctions on Iran and Syria.[490]

May 2, 2013   Sec. Defense Chuck Hagel confirms that the Obama administration is reconsidering arming the rebels as a legitimate policy option.[491]

May 9, 2013   Sec. Kerry announces an additional $100 million in humanitarian aid, bringing U.S. donations to $510 million.[492] Sec. Hagel makes comments on Syria at the Washington Institute for Near Eastern Policy.[493]

May 22, 2013   Friends of Syria Group met again today in Amman amid the escalating conflict to encourage opposition leaders to agree to meet with the regime in the Geneva II Accords.[494]

[488]Welker, Miklaszewski, Kube and Connor, "White House: US believes Syrian regime used chemical weapons."

[489]Chuck Hagel, "Statement on Syria," Press Release, April 25, 2013 (online by U.S. Department of Defense), http://www.defense.gov/Speeches/Speech.aspx?SpeechID=1773.

[490]"Fact Sheet: New Executive Order Targeting Foreign Sanctions Evaders," Press Release, May 1, 2012 (Online by U.S. Department of the Treasury), http://www.treasury.gov/press-center/press-releases/Pages/tg1558.aspx.

[491]Lolita Baldor, "Hagel: US rethinking possibly arming rebels," U.S. News, May 2, 2013, http://www.usnews.com/news/politics/articles/2013/05/02/hagel-us-rethinking-possibly-arming-rebels.

[492]Bradley Klapper and Matthew Lee, "U.S. To Provide $100 Million In New Syria Aid For Humanitarian Purposes Only," The Huffington Post, May 8, 2013, http://www.huffingtonpost.com/2013/05/08/us-syria-aid-humanitarian_n_3237964.html.

[493]Chuck Hagel, "Washington Institute for Near East Policy Soref Symposium," Speech, May 9, 2013 (online by U.S. Department of Defense), http://www.defense.gov/Speeches/Speech.aspx?SpeechID=1777.

[494]"Friends of Syria meet as conflict escalates," The Daily Star, May 22, 2013, http://www.dailystar.com.lb/News/Middle-East/2013/May-22/217973-friends-of-syria-meet-as-conflict-escalates.ashx.

June 12, 2013	U.S. Departments of State, Commerce and Treasury ease sanctions in Syrian opposition-held areas.[495]
June 13, 2013	Pres. Obama authorizes providing weapons to the Syrian opposition because the administration claims it has conclusive evidence that Assad used weapons on a small scale against his own people.[496]
June 17, 2013	At a G-8 Summit in Northern Ireland, Pres. Obama announces an additional $300 million in humanitarian aid, bringing the U.S. total to $815 million.[497]
June 22, 2013	Friends of Syria Group meets in Doha to discuss arming rebels.[498]
June 26, 2013	Amb. Rice, in her last comments as U.S. ambassador to the UN, calls inaction on Syria "a stain" on the Security Council's reputation: "The council's inaction on Syria is a moral and strategic disgrace that history will judge harshly."[499]
August 26, 2013	Sec. Kerry makes remarks to the press condemning the attacks in Ghouta and confirming U.S. consultation with allies and consideration of policy options.[500]
August 29, 2013	VP Biden demonstrated his resolve against the military option by saying that if Pres. Obama led an intervention in Syria without Congressional authorization, he would move to impeach him.[501]

[495]"Sanctions Eased for Syrian Opposition," Media Note, June 12, 2013 (online by the U.S. Department of State, Office of the Spokesperson), http://www.state.gov/r/pa/prs/ps/2013/06/210577.htm.

[496]Lee and Julie Pace, "Obama Authorizes Sending Weapons To Syrian Rebels"; "Statement by Deputy National Security Advisor for Strategic Communications Ben Rhodes on Syrian Chemical Weapons Use," Press Release, June 13, 2013 (online by the White House Office of the Press Secretary), http://www.whitehouse.gov/the-press-office/2013/06/13/statement-deputy-national-security-advisor-strategic-communications-ben-.

[497]"FACT SHEET: President Obama Increases Humanitarian Assistance to Syrians," Press Release, June 17, 2013 (online by the White House Office of the Press Secretary), http://www.whitehouse.gov/the-press-office/2013/06/17/fact-sheet-president-obama-increases-humanitarian-assistance-syrians.

[498]"'Friends of Syria' debate arming rebels," Al Jazeera, June 22, 2013, http://www.aljazeera.com/news/middleeast/2013/06/201362263944556379.html.

[499]"Susan Rice: Syria inaction a 'stain' on security council," BBC News, June 26, 2013, http://www.bbc.com/news/world-us-canada-23057745.

[500]John Kerry, "Remarks on Syria," Remarks, August 26, 2013 (online by U.S. Department of State), http://www.state.gov/secretary/remarks/2013/08/213503.htm.

[501]Conor Friedersdorf, "Joe Biden's Case That Waging War Without Congress Is an Impeachable Offense," The Atlantic, August 29, 2013, http://www.theatlantic.com/politics/archive/2013/08/joe-bidens-case-that-waging-war-without-congress-is-an-impeachable-offense/279160/.

August 30, 2013	The Obama administration declares "with high confidence" that the Assad regime carried out the chemical attacks in Ghouta.[502] Sec. Kerry says that the U.S. is weighing options while it is in communication with the UN, U.S. allies, and "the American people."[503]
August 31, 2013	In a press conference, Pres. Obama publicly opts for a targeted military strike against the Assad regime in response to the chemical attack and announces that he will seek Congressional authorization for the use of force.[504]
September 3, 2013	Following his announcement, Pres. Obama meets with Congressional leaders at the White House to discuss the use of force.[505] Sec. Kerry, Sec. Hagel, and Gen. Dempsey testify at the Senate Foreign Relations committee about the possible authorization of U.S. military action against the Syrian government.[506] Sec. Hagel comments, "A refusal to act would undermine the credibility of America's other security commitments – including the President's commitment to prevent Iran from acquiring a nuclear weapon. The word of the United States must mean something."[507]
September 4, 2013	Pres. Obama insists that the U.S. "did not set a red line; the world set a red line."[508] Sec. Kerry reiterates this sentiment almost verbatim in his testimony before the House Foreign Affairs Committee.[509]
September 6, 2013	U.S. Permanent Representative to the United Nations Samantha Power discussed the Assad regime's use of chemical

[502]"Government Assessment of the Syrian Government's Use of Chemical Weapons on August 21, 2013."

[503]John Kerry, "Statement on Syria," Press Release, August 30, 2013 (online by U.S. Department of State), http://www.state.gov/secretary/remarks/2013/08/213668.htm.

[504]Barack Obama, "Statement by the President on Syria," Press Release, August 31, 2013 (online by the White House Office of the Press Secretary), http://www.whitehouse.gov/the-press-office/2013/08/31/statement-president-syria.

[505]Barack Obama, "Remarks by the President Before Meeting with Members of Congress on the Situation in Syria," Press Release, September 3, 2013 (online by the White House Office of the Press Secretary), http://www.whitehouse.gov/the-press-office/2013/09/03/remarks-president-meeting-members-congress-situation-syria; Megan Slacks, "President Obama Meets with Congressional Leaders on Syria," The White House Blog, September 3, 2013, http://www.whitehouse.gov/blog/2013/09/03/president-obama-meets-congressional-leaders-syria.

[506]"FULL TRANSCRIPT: Kerry, Hagel and Dempsey testify at Senate Foreign Relations Committee hearing on Syria."

[507]Chuck Hagel, Statement on Syria before the Senate Foreign Relations Committee.

[508]Robert, "Obama seeks global backing on Syria: 'I didn't set a red line. The world did.'"

[509]John Kerry, Testimony before the House Foreign Affairs Committee, Syria: Weighing the Obama Administration's Response, Hearing, September 4, 2013, Available online at: http://www.state.gov/secretary/remarks/2013/09/213787.htm.

weapons against Syrian civilians and the need for a limited military response.[510] Also, the president issues a joint statement on Syria with ten other nations condemning the Ghouta attack and repeating its support of non-proliferation.[511] By September 9th, thirty-seven more countries join in supporting the statement.[512] Sec. Kerry publishes an op-ed in The Huffington Post in which he advocates for limited military action in Syria as someone who is "informed, not imprisoned" by the military analogies of Vietnam and Iraq.[513]

September 7, 2013   In his weekly address, President Obama makes the case for limited and targeted military action to hold the Assad regime accountable for its violation of international norms prohibiting the use of chemical weapons.[514]

September 9, 2013   Pres. Obama continues his support for the limited military strike.[515] Ambassador Rice lays out the case for the damage that would be done to our national security and that of our partners and allies should we fail to respond to enforce the longstanding international norm against the use of chemical weapons.[516] Former Sec. of State Clinton also agrees with the President's remarks, stating that she would "continue to support his efforts, and I hope the Congress will as well."[517]

---

[510]Samantha Powers, "Remarks by Ambassador Samantha Power, U.S. Permanent Representative to the United Nations, on Syria at the Center for American Progress, Washington D.C.," Statement, September 6, 2013 (online by U.S. Mission to the United Nations), http://usun.state.gov/briefing/statements/213901.htm.

[511]"Joint Statement on Syria," Press Release, September 6, 2013 (online by the White House Office of the Press Secretary), http://www.whitehouse.gov/the-press-office/2013/09/06/joint-statement-syria.

[512]"Statement on Additional Countries in Support of September 6 Joint Statement on Syria," Press Release, September 9, 2013 (online by the White House Office of the Press Secretary), http://www.whitehouse.gov/the-press-office/2013/09/09/statement-additional-countries-support-september-6-joint-statement-syria.

[513]John Kerry, "A Yes Vote of Conscience for the World's Red Line," The Huffington Post, September 6, 2013, http://www.huffingtonpost.com/johnkerry/syria-red-line-vote-conscience_b_3879304.html.

[514]Barack Obama, "Weekly Address: Calling for Limited Military Action in Syria," Press Release, September 7, 2013 (online by the White House Office of the Press Secretary), http://www.whitehouse.gov/the-press-office/2013/09/07/weekly-address-calling-limited-military-action-syria.

[515]Alicia Oken, "Weekly Wrap Up: Syria and the G-20," The White House Blog, September 6, 2013, http://www.whitehouse.gov/blog/2013/09/06/weekly-wrap-9613-situation-syria.

[516]Caitlin Hayden, "National Security Advisor Susan Rice Speaks on Syria," The White House Blog, September 9, 2013, http://www.whitehouse.gov/blog/2013/09/09/national-security-advisor-susan-rice-speaks-syria.

[517]Hillary Clinton, "Former Secretary of State Clinton's Statement on Syria," Speech, September 9, 2013 (online by the White House Office of the Press Secretary), http://www.whitehouse.gov/photos-and-video/video/2013/09/09/former-secretary-state-clintons-statement-syria.

September 10, 2013 — In response to the Ghouta chemical attacks, Pres. Obama gives a speech in which he favors a Russian-brokered diplomatic solution over a military option in response for Syria crossing the "red line."[518] The President asks Congress to hold off on the vote while the first round of diplomatic engagement played out.[519] Sec. Kerry, Sec. Hagel, and Gen. Dempsey visit the House Armed Services Committee advocating the Geneva II process and asserting that the timeline for handing over chemical weapons "cannot be a delaying tactic."[520] Sec. Hagel concurs with Sec. Kerry in his testimony before the House committee and outlines reason for U.S. action.[521] Sec. Kerry also gives an interview regarding U.S. options on Syria, reiterating his views from the House committee hearing.[522]

September 14, 2013 — In his weekly address, Pres. Obama says there is the possibility for a diplomatic solution in Syria, partially because of the "credible threat of U.S. military force."[523] The White House issues a statement applauding the progress made with Russia on the agreement on the Framework for the Elimination of Syrian Chemical Weapons.[524]

September 15, 2013 — VP Biden receives criticism for using Obama's negotiated political solution with Russia and Syrian officials as a "vic-

[518]Barack Obama, "Remarks by the President in Address to the Nation on Syria," Press Release, September 10, 2013 (online by the White House Office of the Press Secretary), http://www.whitehouse.gov/the-press-office/2013/09/10/remarks-president-address-nation-syria.

[519]Jeff Zeleny and Arlette Saenz, "Obama Asks Congress to Delay Vote on Syria," *ABC News*, September 10, 2013, http://abcnews.go.com/blogs/politics/2013/09/obama-asks-congress-to-delay-vote-on-syria/.

[520]John Kerry, Testimony before the House Armed Services Committee, *Proposed Authorization to Use Military Force in Syria*, Hearing, September 10, 2013, Available online at: http://www.state.gov/secretary/remarks/2013/09/214028.htm.

[521]Chuck Hagel, Testimony before the House Armed Services Committee, *Proposed Authorization to Use Military Force in Syria*, Hearing, September 10, 2013, Available online at: http://www.defense.gov/Speeches/Speech.aspx?SpeechID=1803.

[522]John Kerry, interview by Lara Setrakian, Syria Deeply, September 10, 2013, http://www.state.gov/secretary/remarks/2013/09/214049.htm.

[523]Barack Obama, "Weekly Address: Pursuing a Diplomatic Solution in Syria," Press Release, September 14, 2013 (online by the White House Office of the Press Secretary), http://www.whitehouse.gov/the-press-office/2013/09/14/weekly-address-pursuing-diplomatic-solution-syria.

[524]Barack Obama, "Statement by the President on U.S.-Russian Agreement on Framework for Elimination of Syrian Chemical Weapons," Press Release, September 14, 2013 (online by the White House Office of the Press Secretary), http://www.whitehouse.gov/the-press-office/2013/09/14/statement-president-us-russian-agreement-framework-elimination-syrian-ch.

	tory lap" for the administration in one of the U.S.'s most important caucus states.[525]
September 19, 2013	Sec. Kerry states that the UN Sellstrom Report on Syria's chemical weapon use confirms and strengthens the U.S. report issued weeks before, emphasizing the need for international action against the Assad regime.[526]
September 24, 2013	Pres. Obama announces that the U.S. will provide $339 million in additional humanitarian aid, bringing the total aid given by this point to $1.4 billion. Sec. Kerry holds a meeting with SNC Chairman Jarba.
September 26, 2013	At the Friends of the Syrian People Ministerial, Sec. Kerry reiterates U.S. commitment to the diplomatic process and thanks the Syrian opposition for agreeing to participate in Geneva II.[527]
September 27, 2013	UN Security Council Resolution 2118 is passed demanding that Syria remove its chemical weapons in accordance with the OPCW's framework.[528]
October 22, 2013	UK FM Hague speaks on behalf of the Friends of Syria after meeting of core group in London endorsing the Geneva process and reiterating that there is no place for Assad in Syria's future.[529]
October 31, 2013	In a press statement, Sec. Kerry applauds the completion of the first milestone in eliminating Syria's chemical weapons and states that the U.S. will show its continued financial and political support for the mission.[530]
November 25, 2013	Sec. Kerry issues a press statement thanking Special Representative Brahimi for his agreement to participate in the Geneva talks and underscoring the importance of a diplomatic solution.[531]

[525]Burns, "Joe Biden credits Obama on Syria."

[526]John Kerry, "Remarks to the Press on Syria," Press Release, September 19, 2013 (online by U.S. Department of State), http://www.state.gov/secretary/remarks/2013/09/214441.htm.

[527]John Kerry, "Remarks at the Friends of the Syrian People Ministerial," Press Release, September 26, 2013 (online by U.S. Department of State), http://www.state.gov/secretary/remarks/2013/09/214830.htm.

[528]United Nations Security Council Resolution 2118, September 27, 2013, Available online at: http://unscr.com/en/resolutions/doc/2118.

[529]William Hague, "'London 11' meeting on Syria," Press Release, October 22, 2013 (online by the U.K. Foreign & Commonwealth Office), https://www.gov.uk/government/news/london-11-meeting-on-syria.

[530]John Kerry, "Progress Eliminating Syria's Chemical Weapons Program," Press Release, October 31, 2013 (online by U.S. Department of State), http://www.state.gov/secretary/remarks/2013/10/216143.htm.

[531]John Kerry, "Geneva Conference on Syria," Press Release, November 25, 2013 (online by U.S. Department of State), http://www.state.gov/secretary/remarks/2013/11/218045.htm.

December 11, 2013	U.S. and Britain suspend non-lethal aid after a raid on a Free Syrian Army warehouse by the Islamic Front.[532]
January 23, 2014	Kerry promises protection to Syrian minorities if they abandon Assad, not by American troops but by the many other countries "who would be willing" to go there as peacekeepers.[533]
January 27, 2014	Congress discretely approves light weapons to flow to "moderate" rebels.[534]
January 28, 2014	News of Congress' approval of lethal aid disrupts Geneva II talks.[535]
January 30, 2014	State Dept. Spokesperson Jen Psaki accuses Syria of "dragging its feet" on the removal of chemical weapons. Sec. Hagel echoes this disenchantment with the regime, stating, "I do not know what the Syrian government's motives are — if this is incompetence — or why they are behind in delivering these materials."[536]
January 31, 2014	Sec. Kerry warns Assad that it could face UNSC punishment for failure to comply with the chemical weapons removal framework.[537] "Friends of Syria," which includes the U.S., blames the failure of Geneva II on Assad's unwillingness to negotiate.[538]
February 1, 2014	Jen Psaki denies Syrian FM al Moualem's claim that the U.S. sought direct negotiations with the Syrian regime, circumventing UN intermediaries.[539]

[532]"US and UK suspend non-lethal aid for Syria rebels," *BBC News,* December 11, 2013, http://www.bbc.com/news/world-middle-east-25331241.

[533]Julian Pecquet, "Kerry promises protection for Syrian minorities," *The Hill,* January 23, 2014, http://thehill.com/policy/international/196269-kerry-promises-protection-for-syrian-minorities.

[534]Mark Hosenball, "Congress secretly approves U.S. weapons flow to 'moderate' Syrian rebels," *Reuters,* January 27, 2014, http://www.reuters.com/article/2014/01/27/us-usa-syria-rebels-idUSBREA0Q1S320140127.

[535]Anne Barnard and Nick Cumming-Bruce, "Syrian Talks Disrupted by Congress's Approval of Aid to Rebels," *The New York Times,* January 28, 2014, http://www.nytimes.com/2014/01/29/world/middleeast/syria.html?_r=0.

[536]"U.S. accuses Syria of 'dragging its feet' on chemical weapons," *Raw Story,* January 30, 2014, http://www.rawstory.com/rs/2014/01/u-s-accuses-syria-of-dragging-its-feet-on-chemical-weapons/.

[537]Paul Richter, "Kerry warns Syria of possible U.N. action over chemical arms delay," *Los Angeles Times,* January 31, 2014, http://www.latimes.com/world/worldnow/la-fg-wn-kerry-syria-chemical-arms-20140131-story.html.

[538]Khaled Oweis, "'Friends of Syria' blame Assad for holding up peace talks," *Reuters,* January 31, 2014, http://www.reuters.com/article/2014/01/31/us-syria-crisis-talks-friends-idUSBREA0U18E20140131.

[539]"U.S. denies it sought direct negotiations with Syria in Geneva," *Reuters,* February 1, 2014, http://www.reuters.com/article/2014/02/02/us-syria-crisis-talks-idUSBREA0T0W420140202.

February 4, 2014	During a hearing before the House Intelligence Committee, Mr. Clapper said that Mr. Assad had grown stronger over the past year "by virtue of his agreement to remove the chemical weapons." This NYTimes article also notes that though Pres. Obama claimed "Assad must go" in mid-2011, this language has dropped from his recent statements.[540]
February 6, 2014	U.S. Ambassador to the UN Samantha Power questions the sincerity of Assad regime's intentions in releasing civilians trapped in Homs after UN-encouraged deal.[541]
February 7, 2014	Sec. of Homeland Security Jeh Johnson says Syria becoming a greater threat to U.S. security due to threat that jihadis will return to the U.S. to launch attacks.[542]
February 11, 2014	Pres. Obama reiterates that there is "no military solution in Syria" but that peace talks are stalling.[543]
February 14, 2014	Given the failure of Geneva II, Pres. Obama again opens up to suggestions of policy options, but few seem forthcoming.[544]
February 15, 2014	Pres. Obama threatens to "apply more pressure" to the Assad regime after Geneva talks end fruitless.[545]
February 16, 2014	Sec. Kerry issues a statement blaming the stalled Geneva negotiations on the Syrian regime but ensures that the U.S. remains committed to a diplomatic solution.[546] He also insisted that there is talks will not move forward if Assad believes he has a place in Syria's future.[547]

[540]Gordon and Mazzetti, "U.S. Spy Chief Says Assad Has Strengthened His Hold on Power."

[541]Erika Solomon and Michelle Nichols, "U.N. welcomes reported Homs humanitarian deal, U.S. skeptical," *Reuters*, February 6, 2014, http://www.reuters.com/article/2014/02/06/us-syria-crisis-idUSBREA151E020140206.

[542]"Homeland Security Secretary: Syria Conflict a Threat to U.S.," *CBS News*, February 7, 2014, http://www.cbsnews.com/news/homeland-security-secretary-syria-conflict-a-threat-to-united-states/.

[543]"Obama: Right Now No Military Solution in Syria," News Conference, February 11, 2014 (online by Bloomberg TV), http://www.bloomberg.com/video/obama-right-now-no-military-solution-in-syria-oJtwI5SOSdWLyb4CUgM_ag.html.

[544]"Kerry says Obama seeks Syria options, none presented yet," *Reuters*, February 14, 2014, http://www.reuters.com/article/2014/02/14/us-syria-crisis-usa-idUSBREA1D0NC20140214?utm_source=Sailthru&utm_medium=email&utm_term=*Mideast%20Brief&utm_campaign=Mideast%20Brief%202-14-2014.

[545]Richard Spencer, "Syria: Barack Obama threatens to 'apply more pressure' on Assad regime," *The Telegraph*, February 15, 2014, http://www.telegraph.co.uk/news/worldnews/middleeast/syria/10640895/Syria-Barack-Obama-threatens-to-apply-more-pressure-on-Assad-regime.html.

[546]John Kerry, "Geneva Conference and Situation in Syria," Press Release, February 16, 2014 (online by U.S. Department of State), http://www.state.gov/secretary/remarks/2014/02/221702.htm.

[547]"Kerry insists no place for Assad in Syria's future," *Reuters*, January 17, 2014, http://www.reuters.com/article/2014/01/17/us-syria-crisis-kerry-idUSBREA0G14A20140117.

February 17, 2014	Sec. Kerry accuses Russia and Iran of effectively undermining Syrian peace talks by stepping up military support and aid to the regime while Assad tries to "double down" on a military victory.[548]
February 18, 2014	U.S. decides to reconsider options for Syria after failure of Geneva II.[549]
February 20, 2014	The United States and its European and Arab allies have set up regulations that establish a unified way to provide aid to rebel groups. Categories include groups that should receive arms and other assistance, groups that are excluded due to extremist ties, and those that require further discussion.[550]
February 22, 2014	UN Security Council Resolution 2139 is passed calling upon the different parties in Syria to allow greater access for humanitarian aid.[551]
March 4, 2014	Pres. Obama's FY2015 budget asks Congress for $1.5 billion dedicated to deal with the humanitarian crisis in Syria.[552] Undersecretary of the Treasury David Cohen releases a statement calling Kuwait, a U.S. ally, the "epicenter of fundraising for terrorist groups in Syria."[553]
March 5, 2014	The U.S. restricts Syria's ambassador to the UN to keep his movements to a 25-mile radius around New York.[554] The U.S.

---

[548]Simon Denyer, "Kerry says Russia and Iran undermining Syria peace talks," *The Washington Post,* February 17, 2014, http://www.washingtonpost.com/world/kerry-says-russia-undermines-syria-talks/2014/02/17/c6e88386-979c-11e3-ae45-458927ccedb6_story.html.

[549]Entous and Barnes, "U.S. Revisits Options on Syria as Talks Stall."

[550]Karen DeYoung, "U.S., allies agree on standards for which opposition groups in Syria will receive aid," *The Washington Post,* February 20, 2014, http://www.washingtonpost.com/world/national-security/us-allies-agree-on-standards-for-which-opposition-groups-in-syria-will-receive-aid/2014/02/20/7b5b8b02-9a53-11e3-b931-0204122c514b_story.html.

[551]"Security Council Unanimously Adopts Resolution 2139 (2013) to Ease Aid Delivery to Syrians, Provide Relief from 'Chilling Darkness,'" United Nations, Meetings Coverage and Press Releases, February 22, 2014, http://www.un.org/press/en/2014/sc11292.doc.htm.

[552]Julian Pecquet, "Obama budget carves out $1.5 billion for Syria," *The Hill,* March 4, 2014, http://thehill.com/policy/international/199847-obama-budget-carves-out-15-billion-for-syria.

[553]"Remarks of Under Secretary for Terrorism and Financial Intelligence David Cohen before the Center for a New American Security on 'Confronting New Threats in Terrorist Financing,'" March 4, 2014 (online by U.S. Department of the Treasury), http://www.treasury.gov/press-center/press-releases/Pages/jl2308.aspx.

[554]"U.S. restricts movements of Syria's U.N. envoy Ja'afari," *Reuters,* March 5, 2014, http://www.reuters.com/article/2014/03/05/us-syria-crisis-usa-un-idUSBREA2429I20140305?utm_source=Sailthru&utm_medium=email&utm_term=*Mideast%20Brief&utm_campaign=Mideast%20Brief%203-6-14.

	Ambassador to the UN Power accuses the Syrian government on "stonewalling" on the chemical removal timeline.[555]
March 17, 2014	Daniel Rubenstein replaces Robert Ford as U.S. Special Envoy to Syria.[556]
March 18, 2014	U.S. State Department notifies the Syrian Embassy in D.C. that it must close by the end of the month.[557]
March 24, 2014	The U.S. resumes aid to the Syrian opposition after grave mismanagement of materials caused the U.S. to suspend aid.[558] Sec. Kerry makes remarks with OPCW Director-General Uzumcu before their meeting supporting the removal framework.[559]
March 26, 2014	Whatever facade remained of a unified congressional and executive foreign policy stance was shattered in a heated debate on the floor of the Senate Foreign Relations Committee.[560]
April 1, 2014	The Senate Foreign Relations Committee approved a non-binding measure that requires the Obama administration to provide Congress with an updated humanitarian strategy for Syria within 90 days.[561] The House followed suit.[562]

[555]Louis Charbonneau, "U.S. accuses Syria of stonewalling on chemical arms plants," *Reuters,* March 5, 2014, http://www.reuters.com/article/2014/03/06/us-syria-crisis-chemical-usa-idUS-BREA2501R20140306?utm_source=Sailthru&utm_medium=email&utm_term=*Morning%20Brief&utm_campaign=MB.03.06.2014.

[556]Michael Gordon, "Kerry Announces U.S. Representative to Syrian Opposition," *The New York Times,* March 17, 2014, http://www.nytimes.com/2014/03/18/world/middleeast/kerry-announces-us-representative-to-syrian-opposition.html?ref=middleeast&utm_source=Sailthru&utm_medium=email&utm_term=*Mideast%20Brief&utm_campaign=Mideast%20Brief%203-18-14.

[557]"U.S. Relations with Syria," Fact Sheet, U.S. Department of State, March 20, 2014, http://www.state.gov/r/pa/ei/bgn/3580.htm.

[558]Gordon Lubold, "U.S. Readies New Syria Aid, *Foreign Policy,* March 25, 2014, http://foreignpolicy.com/2014/03/25/u-s-readies-new-syria-aid/.

[559]John Kerry, "Remarks With OPCW Director-General Ahmet Uzumcu Before Their Meeting," Press Release, March 24, 2014 (online by U.S. Department of State), http://www.state.gov/secretary/remarks/2014/03/223845.htm.

[560]Karen DeYoung, "Senators unleash criticism of Obama administration over handling of war in Syria," *The Washington Post,* March 26, 2014, http://www.washingtonpost.com/world/national-security/senators-unleash-criticism-of-obama-administration-over-handling-of-war-in-syria/2014/03/26/dd4da610-b524-11e3-8cb6-284052554d74_story.html.

[561]Julian Pecquet, "Senate panel calls for new US strategy for Syria," *Al Monitor's Congress Pulse,* April 1, 2014, http://www.al-monitor.com/pulse/originals/2014/04/senate-strategy-syria-us-calls.html.

[562]*Calling for an end to attacks on Syrian civilians and expanded humanitarian access,* H.Res.520, 113th Congress, 2014, https://www.govtrack.us/congress/bills/113/hres520/text.

April 13, 2014	The U.S. Ambassador to UN Samantha Power states that reports regarding a new, but limited, poison gas attack have been unsubstantiated.[563] The claims from either side have not yet been substantiated. Nevertheless, the U.S. will do what is necessary to "establish what has happened and then consider possible steps in response."
April 18, 2014	Reports surface that the U.S. and Saudi Arabia have supplied Syrian rebel groups with a number of American anti-tank missiles for the first time in a pilot program.[564]
April 21, 2014	U.S. cites "indications" that confirm allegations that the Syrian government used a toxic agent to attack a rebel-controlled area in Kafr Zeita, yet the reports were not yet substantiated.[565]
April 28, 2014	Sec. of Homeland Security Jeh Johnson announces, "Syria has become a matter of homeland security" due to the growing threat of jihadism returning to the United States.[566]
May 5, 2014	The State Department announces the delivery of an additional $27 million in non-lethal aid. It also announces that the U.S. will allow the Syrian National Coalition to establish a foreign mission in Washington D.C. However, members do not receive diplomatic immunity and do not replace the Syrian embassy.[567]
May 7, 2014	Pres. Obama notifies Congress of the extension of the state of national emergency with respect to Syria beyond May 11, 2014.[568]

[563]Loveday Morris, "U.S. looks into new Syria chemical weapons attack claims," *The Washington Post*, April 13, 2014, http://www.washingtonpost.com/world/us-looks-into-new-syria-chemical-weapons-attack-claims/2014/04/13/548d898d-ef9d-48c6-b55c-6b2eec65c0a0_story.html.

[564]Knickmeyer, Abi-Habib and Entous, "Advanced U.S. Weapons Flow to Syrian Rebels."

[565]Anne Gearan, "U.S. cites 'indications' toxic chemical was used in Syria attack," *The Washington Post*, April 21, 2014, http://www.washingtonpost.com/world/national-security/us-cites-indications-toxic-chemical-was-used-in-syria-attack/2014/04/21/78a8592c-c987-11e3-93eb-6c0037dde2ad_story.html.

[566]Susan Jones, "Jeh Johnson: 'Syria Has Become a Matter of Homeland Security,'" *CNS News*, April 28, 2014, http://www.cnsnews.com/news/article/susan-jones/jeh-johnson-syria-has-become-matter-homeland-security.

[567]"Syrian opposition will have foreign mission in US," *BBC News*, May 5, 2014, http://www.bbc.com/news/world-us-canada-27287650?utm_source=Sailthru&utm_medium=email&utm_term=*Morning%20Brief&utm_campaign=MB%20050614.

[568]"Message to the Congress -- Continuation of the National Emergency with respect to Syria," Press Release, May 7, 2014 (online by the White House Office of the Press Secretary), http://www.whitehouse.gov/the-press-office/2014/05/07/message-congress-continuation-national-emergency-respect-syria.

May 8, 2014	Sec. Kerry welcomes SNC President Jarba to the U.S. for meetings with White House and Congress.[569] Department of Treasury increases sanctions on Russian bank Tempbank as well as Syrian government officials and refineries like Banias Refinery Co. and Homs Refinery Co.[570]
May 12, 2014	Sec. Kerry told members of the Syrian opposition in a private meeting that the U.S. "wasted a year" by not working together as the international community to defeat Assad.[571]
May 14, 2014	Pres. Obama and NSA Rice meet with SNC Pres. Jarba as a show of support for the opposition, especially amid concerns that lethal weapons may make it into the wrong hands.[572] The Treasury Department announces sanctions against two "specially designated global terrorists" in Syria for their support of al-Qaeda.[573]
May 15, 2014	Rebels stated that the Southern Front strategy suggested by the U.S. government has failed. The Friends of Syria group meets for the first time since January and condemns Assad's "parody" of elections. Kerry states, "We have to redouble our efforts, all of us, in support of the moderate opposition in order to bring about a peaceful resolution that the people of Syria want."[574]
May 22, 2014	China and Russia veto a UN Security Council Resolution that would make Assad stand trial before the International Criminal Court.[575] Amb. Samantha Power responds, "The

[569]John Kerry, "Remarks With Syrian Opposition Coalition President Ahmad al-Jarba Before Their Meeting," Remarks, May 8, 2014 (online by U.S. Department of State), http://www.state.gov/secretary/remarks/2014/05/225781.htm.

[570]"Treasury Sanctions Syrian Regime Officials and Supporters," Press Release, May 8, 2014 (online by the U.S. Department of the Treasury, Press Center), http://www.treasury.gov/press-center/press-releases/Pages/jl2391.aspx.

[571]Josh Rogin, "Exclusive: Kerry Told Syrian Rebels 'We Wasted a Year' in Fight Against Assad," *The Daily Beast*, May 12, 2014, http://www.thedailybeast.com/articles/2014/05/12/exclusive-kerry-told-syrian-rebels-we-wasted-a-year-in-fight-against-assad.html.

[572]"Obama meets Syria opposition leader Jarba," *Al Jazeera*, May 14, 2014, http://www.aljazeera.com/news/middleeast/2014/05/obama-meets-syria-opposition-leader-jarba-201451491026774741.html.

[573]"Treasury Designates Al-Qa'ida Leaders In Syria," Press Release, May 14, 2014 (online by the U.S. Department of the Treasury, Press Center), http://www.treasury.gov/press-center/press-releases/Pages/jl2396.aspx.

[574]"'Friends of Syria' vow to boost aid to opposition rebels," *France 24*, May 15, 2014, http://www.france24.com/en/20140515-friends-syria-vow-boost-aid-opposition-rebels-london-usa-uk-assad/.

[575]Ian Black, "Russia and China veto UN move to refer Syria to international criminal court," *The Guardian*, May 22, 2014, http://www.theguardian.com/world/2014/may/22/russia-china-veto-un-draft-resolution-refer-syria-international-criminal-court.

Syrian people will not see justice today. They will see crime, but not punishment. The vetoes today have prevented the victims of atrocities from testifying at the Hague."

May 28, 2014   Pres. Obama announces in his West Point Speech he will give the Syrian opposition greater aid as well as give Syrian people more humanitarian assistance.[576]

June 3, 2014   Robert Ford announced he quit his position as U.S. ambassador to Syria because he could no longer support the Obama administration's policy on Syria.[577]

June 4, 2014   While in Lebanon, Secretary Kerry called the elections that extended Bashar al-Assad's rule by seven years a 'great big zero.' He said that the 'elections were non-elections' and that they would have no bearing on U.S. foreign policy.[578] He announced on his trip to Lebanon that the United States would commit an additional $290 million in humanitarian aid, which brings total U.S. contributions to $2 billion.[579]

June 19, 2014   President Obama gives a speech in which he pins the inefficacy of U.S. policy on the underwhelming military capability of the opposition: "And so we have consistently provided that opposition with support. Oftentimes, the challenge is if you have former farmers or teachers or pharmacists who now are taking up opposition against a battle-hardened regime, with support from external actors that have a lot at stake, how quickly can you get them trained; how effective are you able to mobilize them. And that continues to be a challenge."[580] Yet many in the policy field call this an excuse for U.S. inaction, stating that the majority of the opposition

[576]Barack Obama, "Remarks by the President at the United States Military Academy Commencement Ceremony," Press Release, May 28, 2014 (online by the White House Office of the Press Secretary), http://www.whitehouse.gov/the-press-office/2014/05/28/remarks-president-west-point-academy-commencement-ceremony.

[577]Mick Krever, "Former U.S. Ambassador to Syria Robert Ford: I could no longer 'defend the American policy,'" *Amanpour* (blog), June 3, 2014 (10:48 a.m.), http://amanpour.blogs.cnn.com/2014/06/03/former-u-s-ambassador-to-syria-i-could-no-longer-defend-the-american-policy-robert-ford/.

[578]Liz Sly, "Kerry calls Syria election a 'great big zero,'" *The Washington Post,* June 4, 2014, http://www.washingtonpost.com/world/middle_east/kerry-calls-syria-election-a-great-big-zero/2014/06/04/652a9b93-bc29-4f1a-b701-4e614e98c36a_story.html?wprss=rss_world.

[579]John Kerry, "Press Availability in Beirut, Lebanon," Press Release, June 4, 2014 (online by U.S. Department of State), http://www.state.gov/secretary/remarks/2014/06/227100.htm.

[580]Barack Obama, "Remarks by the President on the Situation in Iraq," Press Release, June 19, 2014 (online by the White House Office of the Press Secretary), http://www.whitehouse.gov/the-press-office/2014/06/19/remarks-president-situation-iraq.

has actually received military training through conscription demands.[581]

June 22, 2014   Pres. Obama said that the notion that a US.-backed moderate Syrian rebel force could have stopped Bashar al-Assad and ISIS is a "fantasy."[582]

June 23, 2014   Sec. Kerry issues a statement lauding the international community for its efforts to eliminate Syria's chemical weapons, which it completed as of this day. Sec. Kerry notes, however, that "our work is not finished" and that more must be done to deal with the use of chlorine in opposition areas, to destroy production facilities, and to address the humanitarian crisis.[583]

June 25, 2014   Sec. Kerry issues a warning after Syrian warplanes strike at ISIS combatants in Iraq. He says, "We've made it clear to everyone in the region that we don't need anything to take place that might exacerbate sectarian divisions that are already at a heightened level of tension," Kerry said, speaking at a meeting of diplomats from NATO nations. "It's already important that nothing take place that contributes to the extremism or could act as a flash point with respects to the sectarian divide."[584]

June 26, 2014   Pres. Obama asks Congress for $500 million to directly equip and train the moderate Syrian opposition; operations would be led by the Department of Defense and will expand a CIA program already in place.[585]

June 27, 2014   Sec. Kerry meets with King Abdullah of Saudi Arabia and Ahmad Jarba to discuss what can be done in Syria to stymy ISIS's advance by cooperating with the moderate opposition.[586]

[581]Glenn Kessler, "Are Syrian opposition fighters 'former farmers or teachers or pharmacists'?"

[582]Talev and Keane, "Obama Says Quickly Arming Syrian Opposition a 'Fantasy.'"

[583]John Kerry, "Removal of Declared Chemical Materials from Syria," Press Release, June 23, 2014 (online by U.S. Department of State), http://www.state.gov/secretary/remarks/2014/06/228302.htm.

[584]"Kerry Warns Mideast Nations After Syria Bombs Iraq," CBS News, June 25, 2014, http://www.cbsnews.com/news/u-s-syria-may-have-launched-airstrikes-in-iraq/.

[585]Karen DeYoung, "Obama asks for authorization to provide direct military training to Syrian rebels," The Washington Post, June 26, 2014, http://www.washingtonpost.com/world/national-security/obama-backs-us-military-training-for-syrian-rebels/2014/06/26/ead59104-fd62-11e3-932c-0a55b81f48ce_story.html.

[586]Ahmed Al Omran and Ellen Knickmeyer, "John Kerry Meets With Saudi King Abdullah, Syrian Opposition Leader Jarba," The Wall Street Journal, June 27, 2014.